PILGRIMS MAKE PROGRESS

D1386930

PILGRIMS MAKE PROGRESS

Devotional meditations illuminated by the
*Bible translations of **Alan Dale** and*
*the wisdom of **Julian of Norwich***

HOWARD BOOTH

First published in 2001 by
KEVIN MAYHEW LTD
Buxhall, Stowmarket, Suffolk, IP14 3BW
Email info@kevinmayhewltd.com

© 2001 Howard Booth

The right of Howard Booth to be identified
as the author of this work has been asserted
by him in accordance with the Copyright,
Designs and Patents Act 1988.

All rights reserved. No part of this publication
may be reproduced, stored in a retrieval system,
or transmitted, in any form or by any means,
electronic, mechanical, photocopying, recording
or otherwise, without the prior written permission
of the publisher.

9 8 7 6 5 4 3 2 1 0

ISBN 1 84003 754 7
Catalogue No. 1500435

Cover design by Jonathan Stroulger
Edited and typeset by Elisabeth Bates

Contents

Foreword

It was when I became the Chairman of the Churches' Council for Health and Healing that I first met Howard Booth. He was at that time the Council's Vice-Chairman and we worked amicably together for a number of years. When he retired he was made one of a small number of distinguished Vice-Presidents. Howard was also at that time the Methodist Churches' Advisor on Health and Healing and he has continued in his retirement to make a significant contribution both through his writing and through teaching and lecturing at conferences and quiet days. I have personal experience of his ability to help and inspire.

Now, once again he has given us a 'down-to-earth but heavenward looking' book of devotional meditations, aimed at moving all who read and ponder them towards that greater wholeness which is so universally needed. I commend it with enthusiasm and personal gratitude.

THE RIGHT REVEREND IAN GRIGGS
(formerly Bishop of Ludlow)

Dedication

I would like to dedicate this book to the people I have been privileged to serve in the following appointments during more than fifty years of pastoral and preaching ministry.

1946	Toft Hill and neighbouring Churches in the then West Auckland Circuit.
1946-48	Longmoor Lane and Balliol Road, Bootle, in the then Liverpool North Circuit.
1948-50	Student at Handsworth College, Birmingham.
1950-52	Preston Clubland Church and Youth Centre.
1952-57	St James' Woolton, Childwall Valley and Huyton Quarry in the then Liverpool (Grove Street and Woolton) Circuit.
1957-64	Yiewsley Central Hall and Iver in the then Uxbridge, Hayes and Yiewsley Circuit.
1964-72	Barking and Superintendent of the then East Ham Mission Circuit.
1972-80	North Harrow and Superintendent of the Harrow Circuit.
1980-85	Workington Trinity and Superintendent of the Workington Circuit.
1985-88	Sturminster Newton and neighbouring churches in the then Stour Valley Circuit (part-time).
1985-90	The then Division of Social Responsibility as Health and Healing Advisor (part-time).
1988	A Supernumerary Minister in the Macclesfield Circuit.

Note – My appointment as Health and Healing Advisor ran over for two years into my retirement. I was then what is known as an active supernumerary.

. . . Jesus was not concerned with proselytising or indoctrination but with human maturity. . . . He gave himself to help ordinary people to live as sons and daughters of God their Father. He didn't want 'yes-men', he wanted people to 'judge of themselves', to know what they believe and to love what they know. Only so can he become for us either Leader or Lord.

Alan Dale in the preface to *New World*

We ought to have three ways of understanding. The first is that we know our Lord God. The second is that we know ourselves. The third is that we humbly know how we ourselves stand as regards our sin and weakness.

Mother Julian as translated by Sheila Upjohn in *All Shall Be Well*

Who would true valour see,
let him come hither;
one here will constant be,
come wind, come weather;
there's no discouragement
shall make him once relent
his first avowed intent
to be a pilgrim.

John Bunyan

Introduction

Three combining factors came together as the motivation to write this book. The first was a kind letter out of the blue thanking me for an earlier devotional guide entitled *Healing Experiences* (published by the Bible Reading Fellowship in 1985). I had also written two other 'prayer starters': *Prayer Tools for Health and Healing* (published by The Grail in 1980) and *Stepping Stones to Christian Maturity* (published by Arthur James Ltd in 1991). They had reached some 15,000 readers and seemed to have proved helpful to ordinary Christian pilgrims seeking to discover and rediscover a meaningful inner life.

The second was the help I had myself received in this pursuit from two different writers separated by many years of history. They are Julian of Norwich and Alan Dale. The blessed Mother Julian was an anchoress attached to the Church of St Julian in King Street, Norwich. On 28 May 1373 she received a vision of the crucifixion of our Lord which then became the basis for a series of meditations which she wrote down over the next twenty years. These were made into a book entitled *Revelations of Divine Love*. Originally known to just a few people, today her book has been translated and is read by millions all over the world. I began to use her writings when I discovered a small devotional booklet entitled *Enfolded in Love*. This was made up of selections of her writings prepared by members of the Julian Shrine in 1980 and edited by Robert Llewellyn, with translations by Sheila Upjohn. This little book proved to be a best-selling devotional guide and I found that the writings spoke to my own heart. A little later I discovered a larger volume, *All Shall Be Well*, which took the whole book, *Revelations of Divine Love*, as the starting point but abridged the text, especially avoiding repetitions, and arranged it in suitable portions for daily readings. This translation from the medieval

English was also the work of Sheila Upjohn. (Both books are published by Darton, Longman & Todd.)

In the 1960s when I was a working Methodist Minister in busy urban and suburban centres I became acquainted with the Bible translations of the late Alan Dale. Selections from the New Testament came first and were entitled *New World* (published by the Oxford University Press in 1967). Then later came selections from the Old Testament entitled *Winding Quest* (published by the Oxford University Press in 1972). These writings made an impact upon my own life and ministry equivalent to a reconversion. Through them the scriptures came alive for me in a totally new way and both books have been my regular companions ever since. I have worn out two copies of *New World* and am now on my third.

It then came to me that another devotional guide might include some direct quotes from both authors to be added at the foot of each of my own pieces. These would be designed to open up the subject and perhaps give it a different slant. They would need to be selected carefully and would not always seem to be directly relevant. Further reflection will, I trust, prove them to be complementary.

The third factor which caused me to attempt this task was entirely different. About two years ago, a very dear friend of mine, the Revd Eric Challoner, was moved to write the story of his own interesting and fascinating life and ministry in an autobiography entitled *It So Happened – From Plough to Pulpit* (published by Fairway Folio in 1998). Eric invited me to write the Foreword which I did with great pleasure. Eric's motivation in writing his book was to share his own 'God-confidence' with his readers in the hope that it would inspire them to have more 'God-confidence' themselves. The book has certainly achieved this objective, judging from its enthusiastic reception and the many letters he has received. I was able to read parts of it as it began to develop and then of course to read the final version with riveting interest and warm appreciation.

It may sound strange then to go on to say that my experience has not been the same. In many ways I wish it had but the truth is that personal faith has always been a struggle with me. I am by nature a doubter and I have struggled throughout my Christian life to discover a theology with which I can feel comfortable and at home. I am not an intellectual as such but I have struggled intellectually with my own personal Christian faith. From time to time I have experienced a sense of unreality in what I have been doing and a kind of dryness within my inner self. But my salvation has been that I cannot escape from Jesus. However far I stray I always come back to him. Who he was and what he did is my sheet anchor. It is this abiding truth which has united Eric and myself and has been at the very basis of our friendship. It is rooted in our united love of, and loyalty to, the person of Jesus. Our common experience would be (I think) that in different ways God has used our somewhat different Christian experiences to help others into an understanding of Jesus that is meaningful and relevant to their own lives. This I believe illustrates the true catholicity of the Christian gospel of good news.

I had no sense of call to write the story of my life but I do have an inward compulsion to tell my own story from time to time in *Pilgrims Make Progress*. So this is what I have done – to open up myself as I have sought to discover an ongoing Christian experience through sometimes the inner turmoil that has been the real me. My sole aim has been to be constructive and to exalt Jesus – but also to be honest and to bear witness to the struggle. I just hope that this makes as much sense to my readers as it does to me.

HOWARD BOOTH

The following are the abbreviations used for locating the quotations from both Alan Dale and Mother Julian as translated by Sheila Upjohn.

WQ *Winding Quest – The Heart of the Old Testament in Plain English.*

NW *New World – The Heart of the New Testament in Plain English.*

RDL *All Shall Be Well – Revelations of Divine Love.*

The author and publishers express their thanks to Darton, Longman & Todd Ltd for permission to use quotations from *All Shall Be Well* by Sheila Upjohn (published in 1992) and to the Oxford University Press for permission to use quotations from *New World* (published in 1967) and *Winding Quest* (published in 1972), both by Alan Dale; also the verses by Rosamund E. Herklots on page 25.

Suggestions for the use of this devotional guide

As you proceed through these devotional meditations you will discover that, from time to time, and in different ways, the importance of the body-mind-spirit relationship is emphasised. My own experience is that the entry into quietness within oneself begins with attention to the body. If we are tense and anxious this will affect how we feel. A great deal has been written about stress and its effects upon the human person. When stress levels are high muscles tighten up; the heart beats faster; blood pressure is raised and adrenalin is poured into the bloodstream. These are the things which happen to us when we are preparing for a 'battle' situation. At such times they are necessary and enable us to react properly to a tight and demanding experience – what the psychologists describe as the *fight and flight* syndrome. If, when the immediate situation is over, our body relaxes to its proper balance then we can proceed to live healthily and happily. What often happens, however, is that stress situations of all kinds tend to leave a permanent legacy behind and the effects of stress are built into our everyday patterns of living. There is a way to respond to this and it can well begin with the practice of physical relaxation via some simple exercises.

Before we proceed to make practical suggestions it needs to be emphasised that stress is a normal experience and it is by discovering how best to respond to the demands life makes upon us that we grow and develop as human persons. It is when our ability to deal with stress proves inadequate that things begin to go wrong and we deteriorate physically often in quite small ways – persistent headaches, discomfort in stomach and bowel areas, general feelings of lassitude and so on.

Another factor is our personal genetic inheritance and the way this has been built on by the kind of parenting we receive, especially in the early years of our lives. We do not all come into the world with the same bank balance. Some of us are more prone to suffer from stress situations than others because our genes are different and our childhood experiences have been less than helpful. I write as one who has throughout his life experienced nervous anxiety. Through the help that I have received – not least from meditative practices – I have been able to get insight and so to cope – but the basic pattern of responses has never left me.

So to return to the simple exercises which I have found helpful as the gateway to helpful meditation and reflection.

1. Shake your hands vigorously as though you are getting rid of water. Try to shake them off your arms! You won't be able to but you will be surprised how nice it feels when the increased circulation makes itself felt.

2. Let your arms swing loosely from the shoulders from side to side. Imagine that they are like an old college scarf and just let the arms flop around you.

3. Do the swimmer's exercise vibrating the arms all the way down from the shoulders. (You have often seen swimmers doing this on TV whilst waiting for the start of a race.)

4. Sit on a firm chair with a secure back and let your head come down slowly on to your chest and then on to each shoulder. Then try moving your head from side to side – but not so aggressively that you rick your neck. Arthritics should be careful about this as indeed about any of these exercise suggestions.

5. Move the shoulders like the wheels of a train. First forward and then backward. Thrust them up as though you are a puppet with cords attached and then let them go. Imagine

you are being pulled down by carrying two heavy bags. As you let them go feel the relief from tension this brings.

6. Now give each part of the body its orders. Bring each limb and section of your body into tension by tightening up all the muscles and then letting them go. Start with the feet and work upwards – legs, thighs, trunk, abdomen, chest and shoulders (there is often a lot of tension here), head and eyes.

7. Link this with controlled breathing. Breathe more slowly and more deeply. Avoid quick and shallow breathing which can cause hyperventilation giving rise to symptoms you may feel are related to heart problems when it is really a matter of improved breathing techniques. Learn to think about your breathing patterns at odd moments in the day.

8. Link all this with your thoughts. Learn to recognise negative thoughts and fears and turn them off. Laugh at yourself. This is a most useful practice! Recognise when unnecessary panic is on the way and deflect it by visualising calm and beautiful scenes. If you have a regular form of anxiety then deliberately face it when you are engaged in relaxation practice.

Much of what I have suggested above can take place within an entirely secular context but we are *pilgrims* who want to make *progress* and so we aim to go further. Nevertheless it is good to begin here. God sets great store by our care of our bodies as part of his creation. Remember that in Jesus 'the word became flesh and dwelt among us' (John 1:14). We are seeking a greater wholeness which can only be realised when we are seeking God's will and purpose for our lives. The chief end of all humankind is *to seek God that we may know him and enjoy him for ever and ever* (The Westminster Confession). Paul reminds us that our bodies are 'the temples of the Holy Spirit' (1 Corinthians 6:19). To discover how to use them better is one way of offering our spiritual worship to the source of all our beings – the living God.

So to turn to our devotional meditations. How may we best use them in order to discover growth and development in our Christian pilgrimage?

1. Allow your mind to be stimulated by the initial reflections. See if their content applies to you in any particular way. Try to formulate one sentence that, in your own mind, sums up what I am trying to say. Decide on a particular memory device to hold the thought in your mind throughout the day.

2. Then turn to the Alan Dale Bible verse. See the connection. It will not always be crystal clear but invite the Holy Spirit to make the connection clear *for you*. It will not be the same for everybody; we are all different and God's message comes home in different ways in relation to our different personalities.

3. Then do the same with the word from the Blessed Mother Julian. So many of her words are totally positive. Hold on to them. Hide them within your heart. Rejoice in them.

4. Then compose your own prayer of response. If it helps write it down in a notebook or even in a margin of the book itself. This will make it completely personal.

5. From yourself and your own needs move out to the needs of others. Just hold them quietly in the presence of God, not making any demands but simply loving them in Jesus. Intercessory prayer is not about trying to make God's mind fit in with ours; it is about getting our minds into line with his.

6. Finally recall your key sentence and your prayer last thing at night before you drift into sleep. This practice can make a contribution to the way you sleep and refreshing sleep is vital for our total wellbeing.

As this book is one in which I share some of my own inner story I feel it right simply to testify to the difference this kind of prayer has made to me.

1. It has helped me to move deeper into what I believe to be the meaning of life. It has shown me the importance of *being* as well as *doing*. I have known a good deal of fragmentation from time to time and, as I have already mentioned, some nervous anxiety. This kind of reflective meditation has helped me to recognise and sort out some of my own drives and basic motivations.

2. I have become more aware of my own need simply to be quiet and to spend time alone. Years ago solitude frightened me. I am still gregarious and would find it hard to live alone but now I enjoy going apart to read, pray and think. The occasional retreat to a monastery or other religious community has helped me in this way.

3. I have discovered that prayer makes a difference to my ability to understand other people. When I have spent time prayerfully thinking about someone I have been involved with through the pastoral encounter, there has come to me a more sensitive awareness of them and their real needs. This has sometimes led to my inviting them just to be quiet with me and the end results have often been helpful to both of us.

Getting to know you _____

When new people are introduced to us we often make the polite reply, 'Pleased to know you.' But in fact we don't know them. Really knowing people takes years of companionship, sharing and honest, open relationships. Knowing God is just the same. We must spend time with him. A Salvation Army lady was seen going into the local Parish Church every morning. Her friends enquired about this habit, wondering if she was thinking of leaving the Army. 'Of course not,' she replied. 'I go there to meet with Jesus and when I'm there I sit down, look at him and he looks at me.'

Those versed in the techniques of spirituality would call this Silent Meditation. No words are used but a presence is felt. In that presence life's questions become clearer. Sometimes there are direct answers but not always. Often you just feel more able to cope with the situations you are facing. To know God completely is not possible. God is clothed in mystery. The great thing is that he wants to show himself to us – and the mists begin to clear when we start to look at Jesus.

One of my boyhood heroes was Edward Wilson of the Antarctic. On that last fateful voyage with Captain Scott he was always happy to take his turn on watch in the crow's nest. Here, high and alone, he could keep watch with his Maker as well as look out for sudden dangers.

My own prayer life was transformed when I stopped using many words and began just to be quiet and discern God's presence. To enable this I was taught to use a Bible verse which I repeated silently to myself until I felt God's presence in and around me. My verse was 'Be still and know that I am God.'

Nobody has ever seen God himself; the beloved Son, who knows his Father's secret thoughts, has made him plain.
(John 1:18, NW, p. 301)

And this is our Lord's will – that we trust and believe, joy and delight, comfort and cheer ourselves (as we can with his grace and help) until the time comes when we see this for certain.
(RDL, Chapter 7)

Forgiveness

Our ability to love God and to love others is dependent upon our own experience of forgiveness. Jesus announced the purpose of his mission in Luke 4:14-19. Part of that proclamation was 'to proclaim liberty to the captives and to set free the oppressed'. The same Greek word is used as the basis of both *forgiveness* and *release* so another perfectly legitimate translation would be . . . 'to proclaim *forgiveness* for prisoners and to *forgive* the oppressed'. Jesus forgave freely when the situation called for this redemptive action. We recall his words to the woman taken in adultery . . . 'neither do I condemn thee, go and sin no more' (John 8:11).

What does forgiveness do? It removes burdens and gives a sense of release. In psychotherapy the word used is *catharsis* – the relieving of fears and problems by bringing them into consciousness or giving them expression. The importance of cathartic experiences is enhanced by their being linked with our relationship with God.

So confession as expressed in the Lord's Prayer and the words of sorrow and regret in the Communion Service is important for our health's sake. There is a volcano at Nevis in the West Indies which used to erupt with a mighty force and bring suffering and havoc to those who lived nearby. For years now there have been no violent eruptions but a series of small puffs of smoke and minor rumblings. These regular releases of energy have taken the place of the former major destructive explosions.

The relevance is clear. As we find release week by week and day by day so we are discovering a greater wholeness. Our Christian lives depend upon our sincerely expressed regret and repentance. Through these means we are forgiven.

Forgive our sins as we forgive,
you taught us, Lord, to pray;
but you alone can grant us grace,
to live the words we say.

Lord, cleanse the depths within our souls,
and bid resentment cease.
Then reconciled to God and man,
our lives will spread your peace.

Rosamund E. Herklots

Here is your clue: God's forgiveness of you is the measure of the forgiveness you must show to others. (Colossians 3:13, NW, p. 290)

And because we are made humble (by this) we are raised high in God's sight, by his grace – and also by repentance, and compassion and true yearning for God. (RDL, Chapter 39)

Soul service _____

Every 5,000 miles my present car needs an oil change; every 10,000 it has to be serviced. So does my photocopier; so does our gas heating boiler. Without servicing there would be a breakdown of some sort and the consequent repair would cost more than the regular service.

Recently I was called in to our medical practice for a 75-plus check-up. Various tests were made and I was asked some simple questions. I am not firing on all cylinders but am well enough to keep going for a bit longer anyway.

What about my soul? Does that need servicing? What is my soul like? Where is it to be found? Difficult questions these. My brain can be located, examined through scans. It is identifiable. It can even be operated on if necessary. But the soul – who know what that is like? Yes, it is a complicated question but try this out for size.

Your soul is you. Who you are. What you are. Your soul is revealed through your patience; your kindness to others. It is the essence of your being which is revealed in the complexity of life's challenges, choices and decisions. It is revealed in your breakdowns of temper; in your unwillingness to face up to a particular challenge. It has to do with your fears and persistent anxiety.

At one period of my life I was fortunate enough to belong to a group which met fortnightly for a simple lunch at the house of a religious community. There were about eight of us from different professions attending different Christian churches. We had no set agenda except ourselves. Each member in turn would introduce some aspect of his or her life which was of concern to them at that time. We would all then share our own thoughts and feelings in response to the one whose turn it was to speak first. We were able to drop our masks and speak to each other in complete confidence. At times it was hard going. It is not easy to bare your soul to others but when you know that you are loved and respected it is possible. Looking back now I realise how helpful it was to me in my own Christian pilgrimage. I greatly missed those regular encounters when the time came for me to move on.

How do I provide for a regular servicing of my soul?

By keeping in close touch with the Creator God and the Redeemer Jesus Christ. It also helps to be able to confide in a trusted friend.

Don't try to do what everybody does. Let God keep your mind alive and ready to think new thoughts.
(Romans 12:2, NW, p. 274)

Truth sees God, wisdom perceives God, and from these two comes a third – holy wondering delight in God which is love.
(RDL, Chapter 44)

Symbols

Peter Marshall was Chaplain to the United States Senate and a distinguished preacher. He died of a heart attack in his forties and afterwards his wife wrote the story of his life which was later made into a film – *A Man Called Peter*. One of its most poignant moments was when she took their young son back to their seaside cottage for the first time after his death. As they went in she saw his sandals and bathrobe and other reminders of his presence. She choked back the tears and expressed her depth of feeling in memorable words: 'Oh memories that bless and burn!'

When we come to the Sacrament of Holy Communion we are presented with symbols – but is that all they are? Theologians have debated this down the ages, wanting to give a special significance to what has become for almost all Christians the central act of worship. Of course they remain bread and wine in their essential components but matter is never static. It is always on the move. But what of sacramental bread and wine? Behind it is the life and death of Jesus who declared, 'I am the bread of life'. The elements are charged with love; brought to life by sacrifice. As we appreciate this again and again his life grows in us. We become new men and women. Strengthened. Revived. Restored.

Peter Firth suggests in *The Love that Moved the Sun*[1] that the common phrase *realising your potential* applies to more than one's physical and mental states. It applies to the whole person – that extraordinary amalgam of body, mind and spirit ...

> Love so amazing, so divine,
> demands my life, my soul, my all.
>
> *Isaac Watts*

1 Published by Darton, Longman and Todd, 1996.

As a man he faced the worst; obedience took him to his death . . . that at the name of Jesus the living and the dead should hail him as Lord.
(Philippians 3:8-9, NW, p. 250)

For it is God's will that we should rejoice with him in our salvation and that we should be cheered and strengthened by it. He wants our soul to delight in its salvation, through his grace. For we are his joy. He delights in us for ever as we shall in him, by his grace.
(RDL, Chapter 23)

A credible faith

We were singing carols and giving out gifts in one of the hospital wards where long-term patients were cared for, most of them elderly. One of my favourite ladies was so racked with arthritis that her head was bound to the iron bed surround so that she could look forward and see what was happening. She beckoned me over as we were leaving. I knew her well and we had conversed many times – and I had often prayed with her. This time she whispered in my ear: 'It takes a bit of believing, doesn't it?'

Now I knew that her faith was very real and a source of great comfort and strength but like many of us do she was passing through a time of doubt. The enormous nature of the claim that God became man in the infant Jesus seemed just for a moment to be incredible – unbelievable. I remember kissing her and saying something like: 'Indeed it does but there is light after darkness.'

In the introduction to his massive book, *On Being a Christian*, the Dutch Roman Catholic theologian, Dr Hans Kung, accepts that, from time to time, personal Christian faith is hard to maintain. He himself finds this so but hopes that out of his struggles others will be helped but, he insists, 'In the end each one for himself alone, quite personally, can be or not be a Christian.' He also suggests that in order to gain faith we must go out on a limb and live it out. The answer to our quest comes in Christian existence, action and conduct.

I recall two quotations which helped me through a difficult time of struggling with doubt. The first was, 'If sometimes we don't get lost there is a chance that we may never find the way.' The second: 'The strongest trees are found in the most exposed place.'

Just think about them. Faith and doubt are not contradictory; they belong together.

'God has abandoned me,' says God's people. 'God has forgotten me!' Can a mother forget her baby, neglect her own son? Yes, she can – but I will not forget you! Look! I have branded your name on my hands. (Isaiah 49:14-16, WQ, p. 291)

For it is his will that we should love him dearly, and trust him humbly and strongly. And he showed this in these gracious words: 'I will hold you securely.' (RDL, Chapter 61)

Special moments _____

I used to go and visit a Franciscan Friar about once a month. He was my spiritual counsellor. My job often involved me in asking different people to undertake voluntary jobs in the life of the Church: Sunday school teachers, youth club leaders, treasurers, and so on. I didn't like that side of my work at all. This came out in one of our sessions as I shared with him how uncomfortable it always seemed to make me. He looked at me knowingly and then responded with words of wisdom which initially I found most disturbing: 'You don't like being rejected, Howard, do you?' He spoke gently but firmly and I suddenly realised how much I associated my self-esteem with my requests always being answered in the affirmative. Indeed our pastoral conversation that day also helped me to see that in order to succeed in my mission I had become manipulative. I played upon the quality of our relationship to get my own way.

Being helped to see this was a moment of insight. Initially hurt, I then saw how true it was and how I had allowed my need for personal fulfilment to get in the way of what was best for the Kingdom of God. I certainly changed the way I went about this particular aspect of my job and I felt much better within myself.

I can recall another time when I felt a special moment of awareness. I was responsible for running a training conference for twelve brother ministers. I did so want it to be a success and had put a great deal of work into the preparation. My anxiety about how things were going showed itself to a number of those present. One night one of them was deputed to see me and tell me that they recognised what was happening inside me and they wanted me to know that *they loved me!* My first reaction was embarrassment but then came a marvellous sense of wellbeing. My self-esteem did not depend on the success of the event. I was loved anyway and all that came afterwards was marvellously relaxed.

Isn't this what happened to doubting Thomas on the day he sought confirmation that Jesus had indeed risen from the dead? When Jesus showed him his hands and his side he realised that it was indeed the Lord. Then came one of those special moments of insight for Thomas. He was released from his unbelief and doubt. Renewed faith took over and he was never the same again (see John 20:24-29).

> *You are no longer outsiders and foreigners in God's world; you are fellow-citizens with all the friends of Jesus everywhere and members of God's family.*
> *(Ephesians 2:19, NW, p. 289)*

> *For he says: 'I will shatter all your vain affections and your vicious pride, and after that I shall gather you up and make you kind and gentle, clean and holy, by joining you to me.'*
> *(RDL, Chapter 28)*

Another Trinity

Most doctors today, at whatever level they practise, would claim to believe in the wholistic approach; some might even choose to spell this word in what might be termed a religious way – *holistic*. But some take it more seriously than others. One doctor I know tells his patients that he would like to get a picture of the whole person by getting to know something about their home and family background. He also enquires about what are the major issues they are thinking about. Then without in any way invading their privacy he sensitively enquires if they build their lives around any kind of faith principle. He really believes that all human beings are a delicate amalgam of body, mind and spirit.

Now I know that my body must be taken care of by eating a balanced diet and by exercise. I know that my mind needs to be stimulated by reading, study and reflection. I realise that I need to express myself and be creative so my mind is enlarged and developed. But what about my spirit?

Some recent research in the USA indicated that people who go to Church to worship God have a better health record than those who don't. Without wishing to build too much on a single piece of research this is just a further piece of evidence that we human beings have been made by our Creator to have a three-fold form of existence which like that other trinity – the Holy Trinity – is indivisible. Each aspect of our being is intimately related to the other. As we find satisfaction in one area the effects are felt throughout the whole person.

A South American explorer was trekking in one of the wildest parts of the country. After travelling for eight hours at a cracking pace through difficult country they pitched tents and settled down for the night. At sun-up the explorer arose and began to prepare for another day's trek. After breakfast he waited for the porters to prepare for their journey but they showed no interest at all and just sat on their haunches. In desperation he sent for the head man and asked him to rouse the men for a start. 'Oh no,' said the head man, 'they can't go yet; they are waiting for their souls to catch up with their bodies!'

So you need to find time to be quiet. To think God thoughts. To discover how you can live life to the full on that very day. If you are to be a whole person you will need to feed your spirit as well as your body and mind.

I am the living bread; the living bread which comes from God himself. ... The bread I give is my life, and I give it for the life of the world.
(John 6:51, NW, p. 315)

These are our foundations in which we have our being, our growth and our fulfilment. For in nature we have our life and our being. And in mercy and grace we have our growth and our fulfilment. These are three properties of one goodness and where one works, all work, in the things which concern us now.
(RDL, Chapter 56)

Silence and stillness

Here is a story from the Desert Fathers: Three brothers wanted to live the Christian life. The first went off to be a peacemaker; the second went off to be a healer; the third went off into the desert and became a monk. But peacemaking and healing are not the easiest of tasks and the two brothers who had gone out into the world were feeling frustrated so they went to see their brother who had become a monk in the desert. The monk decided to act out a parable. He poured some water into a bowl and immediately asked them what they saw. The answer they both gave was 'nothing' because the water was still churning. After a while he asked them to look again. This time the water was still and when they looked they saw themselves.

The meaning was clear. In the midst of their busy lives the brothers out in the world needed the stillness in which they could discover more about themselves. It was the philosopher Pascal who said . . .

> Most of man's troubles come from his not being able to sit quietly in his own room.

Remember there is an essential difference between *silence* and *stillness*. While you need silence in order to be still; stillness is not necessarily part of silence. You can be silent but remain inwardly seething.

St Paul had some sound advice in 1 Thessalonians 4:11 (AV): 'Study to be quiet.'

And Mother Teresa adds her own words of wisdom:

> The fruit of silence is prayer,
> the fruit of prayer is faith.
> The fruit of faith is love,
> the fruit of love is service.

*Make Jesus the centre of your life; and with his help
let your hearts be filled with thankfulness to God.
(Ephesians 3:15, NW, p. 290)*

*All the blessed teachings of our Lord were shown to me
in three ways – that is to say, by bodily sight, by words
formed in the mind and by inward sight. . . . As for
the inward sight I can never tell it fully – so I am led
to say more about it as God will give me grace.
(RDL, Chapter 73)*

Grain in winter

This is the title of a book written by a friend of mine, Donald Eadie.[1] He has a serious spinal illness which has resulted in him having to retire from active work far earlier than would normally have been the case. Donald loved his work and his gifts and abilities had been recognised by significant and important posts. Now he spends most of his time in one room. He does not go out to see people very much but people come to him. Many who come are seeking to find *grain in winter*. They are sometimes fellow sufferers but often they are seekers. People who are looking for a form of spirituality that is acceptable to their minds. They do not want to hear religious clichés. They do not want to be told what to believe. So Donald accepts them just as they are which is exactly what Jesus did and does. He listens to them and shares himself with them. They never go away quite the same – at least that is what I hear from people who are regularly in touch with him.

Donald has invented a revealing phrase to describe such individuals. They are *Saturday people*. Why Saturday? Because between Good Friday and Easter Sunday there was Saturday. Saturday people are those who have passed through the events of Good Friday. They have identified with the suffering Jesus. Now they are on the verge of renewal or resurrection. They may not be orthodox in their beliefs but they have been opened up by honest dialogue and sharing.

On the day I wrote this piece I discovered that an old friend and former colleague, David, had died some eight months before. I had not heard of his passing. He was much younger than I am. As I wrote to his wife I recalled a phrase used by a man who had been influenced by David to begin to relate his

1 Published by The Epworth Press, 1999.

Sunday faith to his midweek working life in a large car-making factory. *I feel switched on,* he told me. Exactly. You are never too old to come to life. Or to discover *grain in winter!*

> *It was the Word that made everything alive; and it was this 'being alive' that has been the Light by which men have found their way. The Light is still shining in the darkness; the Darkness has never put it out.*
> *(John 1:1-3, NW, p. 300)*

> *He is quick to clasp us to himself, for we are his joy and his delight, and he is our salvation and our life.*
> *(RDL, Chapter 79)*

Forgiveness and relationships ____

Two ladies who had belonged to the same Church had not spoken to one another for twenty years. Folk had long since forgotten what it was that caused the rift but they remembered and they could not or would not forgive each other. Then one day at a Communion Service their Minister, who had tried hard to bring about a reconciliation, arranged that, unbeknown to them, they should be guided to a place at the communion rail where they were both together kneeling side by side. Before he gave them the bread and wine the Minister went to them and took them each by the hand and placed them together. 'Whatever happened all those years ago,' he said, 'God has forgiven. Now he expects you to forgive each other.' The tears flowed and they received their communion together and left to take their seats side by side instead of at opposite sides of the church.

The consequences were much wider than the effect upon the two of them. The whole Church felt the impact of that happening. There was renewal. New life. Other hurts were revealed and dealt with.

Today there are many divisions in wider society that could be dealt with if only someone would say: *We are sorry – please forgive us.* One of the ways of trying to help individuals who have been affected by crime is to bring the offender and the offended together in a face-to-face encounter. It doesn't always work but where there is genuine penitence there can be true forgiveness. This can set a chain reaction going just as it did in the case quoted above.

I don't know who first said this but I endorse it: *Forgiveness for Jesus was not just something to do with being God; it said something truly profound about being human.*

The trap is broken; we have escaped! Our help is in God who made earth and sky.
(Psalm 124:7, WQ, p. 208)

And so, by humbly knowing our sins through contrition and grace, we shall be broken from all things that are not like our Lord. Then shall our blessed Saviour wholly heal us and make us one with him.
(RDL, Chapter 78)

Encountering the darkness _____

A good psychotherapist tries to help his or her clients to discover more of the truth about themselves. This must always include a personal exploration of the positive aspects of our being but often the problems lie in coming to terms with the darker side of our nature – what Jung calls *the shadow*.

Gonville Ffrench Beytaugh, who was to become an Anglican Priest and senior figure in the hierarchy, had an unhappy childhood. Living for a time in New Zealand he first became a tramp and a casual labourer. Eventually he went to live in South Africa where a meeting with Alan Paton, the author of *Cry the Beloved Country,* was to change his life's direction. Put simply, he was converted and became a Christian. It was this profound experience which led him into the priesthood where he rose rapidly to the position of Dean of Johannesburg. Conflict with the government over apartheid brought him a five-year prison sentence which was quashed on appeal but meant that he was deported to England. When he arrived he had no money and no job. He felt utterly alone and being a depressive by nature found himself passing through a dark valley.

He was eventually appointed to be Rector of St Vedant alias Foster in the City of London. It was a church with only a tiny congregation but soon all that changed. His honesty and openness about his own condition brought many people to his church both for worship and for spiritual direction. He was moving slowly along the road of becoming what, by Divine intention, he truly was.

Coming to terms with inward realities is never easy. A friend of mine once wrote: 'Self-discovery is a painful and sometimes frightening adventure into the darkness of our being . . . but we can sustain the shock if we look at ourselves through the eyes of Christ and know that we are still loved and forgiven. We can take any amount of ourselves if we know that God is like that. We can even begin to love ourselves; and unless and until we do that, we cannot really trust other people to love us.'[1]

He feeds his flock like a shepherd, carrying the lambs in his arms, holding them to his breast and gently leading the ewes heavy with young.
(Isaiah 40:11, WQ, p. 284)

For the soul can do no more than seek, suffer and trust – and this is the work of the Holy Spirit in the soul. And the clearness in finding him comes by his special grace, when it is his will. This seeking with faith, hope and love pleases our Lord, and the finding pleases the soul and fills it with joy.
(RDL, Chapter 10)

1 Betty Hares, *Journeying into Openness*, Shoreline Books.

I want to know the truth _____

The ancient question addressed by Pilate to Jesus: *What is truth?*, is a question we have all asked ourselves at one stage or another in the course of our lives. For many of us the question comes up again and again. Each day on both radio and television issues are presented with representatives from two opposing sides. Unless it is a subject on which you have made up your own mind long ago you can easily be swayed by one side or the other. That, of course, is the object of the exercise. To get you involved. To make you think.

This is an obligation upon all of us who take life seriously. The search for truth must go on and we must all be involved in it. The closed mind is a terminus – nothing passes through. It is like a stagnant pool which needs the refreshment of a flowing stream.

On some matters it is possible to keep an open mind but if we are serious in our own search for truth we must make up our minds upon certain key issues. These will determine our attitudes to so many things so we must make every effort to get it right.

Alan Dale, whose Bible translation quotes we are using in this book, wrote in the Preface to *New World*, 'The clear intention of Jesus was to call everybody to fearless thought as well as to splendid living.' He also quotes the Bible scholar, Dr T. W. Manson: 'Christianity had at its heart a person before it had a creed and a code.'

There you have it. Truth lies in the person of Jesus. Hold fast to him. Breathe in his words. Observe his actions. Take note of how he handled relationships. Then go on searching for the truth. With his help you will find it and live by it.

You who are my friends are like daylight; you must help people to see everything clearly.
(Matthew 5:14, NW, p. 100)

And this has always been a comfort to me, that I chose Jesus as my heaven, by his grace, in this time of Passion and sorrow. And it has been a lesson to me that I should always do this – choose Jesus only as my heaven, in joy and in sorrow.
(RDL, Chapter 19)

Walking frame and springboard

A walking frame and springboard are two very different items of equipment. As I write this piece I have just returned from visiting a friend who, in order to move away from his chair, requires the use of a walking frame. It gives him the support he needs to get from one place to another. It keeps him mobile – on the move. I still visit the swimming pool but there is no springboard in there these days. When I was young I used to love to bounce up and down on the end of the board and then to let it propel me high into the air before I dived into the water.

So far as my faith is concerned I need both a spiritual frame and a spiritual springboard – and often both at the same time. When I am challenged in some aspect of my life, I realise that I do not always have the natural inner strength to face the challenge. Then I feel the need to look to God for support and added strength. Subsequently, when that has been given, I need to be thrust out into that challenging situation. To go in at the deep end. My faith then becomes my springboard.

The disciple Peter had instinctively recognised who Jesus was when he declared in answer to a probing question from Jesus, 'Thou art the Christ, the Son of the Living God.' Later, when challenged, his newly found faith deserted him and he openly denied Jesus. He had been blessed by that inner act of recognition. He did know who Jesus was – but he needed to trust him that one stage more – he needed a springboard to propel him into the heart of the action. Later it happened. Peter the disciple became Peter the apostle who risked his all for his Lord and, according to legend, was crucified upside down. By this time his faith provided both a walking frame and a springboard.

Master every situation with the quietness of heart which Jesus gives us. This is how you were meant to live; not each by himself, but together in company with all the friends of Jesus.
(Colossians 3:15, NW, p. 290)

So I was taught by the grace of God that I should hold steadfastly to the Faith, as I have already understood it, and that I should soberly believe all things shall be well, as our Lord showed me at that time.
(RDL, Chapter 32)

The genuine article

All is not gold that glitters, runs an ancient saying, nor does all *Harris* tweed come from the Isle of Harris. *Genuine* may be the word on the label but not all cloth manufacturers are strictly truthful. Certainly in the past some *Harris* tweed came from Japan!

The claim to be a Christian is used in a variety of ways. For some it simply means that they come from a predominantly Christian country. For others it means that they attend a Church service on odd occasions like Christmas and Easter. However, increasingly in a secular society the differences are being more sharply defined. Many people today claim to have emerged from their superstitious past. They are happy to face the brave new world with a belief in the basic goodness of humanity towards which they claim to make a sincere contribution.

Such people's views are to be respected. We do not help any situation by repeating worn-out dogmas and mindless clichés. But there is such a thing as honest dialogue. This surely is the evangelism for our day: to listen to what others have to say in defence of their own positions and to offer our own basic reasons for continuing to be a person who believes in the Creator God, the Saviour Jesus and God's power alive in the world through the Holy Spirit. This will be all the more convincing if we demonstrate that we and our friends within the Christian community are the genuine article. We think things through; we seek to get into touch with God through the cultivation of our own inner lives – and we seek the mind of Christ in all our social involvements.

'Let the beauty of Jesus be seen in me' is a line from an old-fashioned chorus. But it is still happening. There are those who have sought and do possess *the mind of Christ.* Are you one of them?

If you are always thinking of saving your skin, that's just what you won't do. But, if you forget yourself because you are keen on helping me, even if you lose your life, you will be all right. You will really be yourself.
(Mark 8:35, NW, p. 100)

And by this I saw truly that the inward part is master and king of the outward part. It does not need the will and bidding of the outward part, but all the inward will and intent is settled for ever to be joined with the Lord Jesus.
(RDL, Chapter 19)

Growing old youthfully _____

This may not be such an odd title as it seems. We often hear of an elderly person who is youthful in outlook and who retains vigour of mind and spirit even when the physical effects of ageing begin to show.

It has been pointed out many times that in some mysterious way the effects of the death of Jesus are available to us all. As the familiar hymn puts it: *He died that we might be forgiven, he died to make us good.* He revealed to us on the cross the awful nature of sin and the sheer grandeur of love. Thus out of his death came life.

Then as we proceed through life there come times when we are faced with situations within which we have to allow parts of us to die. Indeed such is the nature of life that we must be prepared to give up willingly what time will demand from us anyway. We are unwise to try to cling to our children – to let them go into their own independent lives will almost always mean that we keep them – but in a different way. We fail to be true to our better selves if we try to hang on to positions of power when it is evident that we should be handing on to others. The creative aspect of all this is that as we die in one aspect of our being so we come alive in another.

I think now of two people. One told me that retirement had brought nothing but sheer misery. He continued to long for and live in his powerful past. Another gave up a senior post long before he need have done. He turned to something totally different. From working mainly with mind and brain he now works with his hands – by the objects he creates he lives. His enthusiasm is infectious.

Doesn't it all come back to Jesus. Those who are linked to him share in the benefits of his death – but not only this. *He lives, he lives, Christ Jesus lives today.* Those who are alive in Christ grow old youthfully.

> *As a man he faced the worst; obedience took him to his death . . . that at the name of Jesus the living and the dead should hail him as Lord, and everybody, everywhere, claim Jesus, God's chosen leader, is Lord! (Philippians 2:5-11, NW, p. 250)*

> *Repentance makes us clean. Compassion makes us ready. And yearning for God makes us worthy. (RDL, Chapter 39)*

Living with tension _____

Physical tension can be destructive if we experience it in long and sustained doses. But not all tension is destructive. Some forms of tension are necessary for our growth and development as persons. They are creative and life giving.

Take the tension between faith and doubt for instance. This is always with us. Faith has given us a foundation upon which we have built our lives but from time to time our faith seems unreal. But all is not lost. Our doubts can give rise to an agonising searching which eventually brings new enlightenment and clearer hope.

It is quite wrong to bury our doubts or to feel guilty about them. We all need the kind of fellowship and deep friendships within which we feel entirely safe to confess our doubts. Years ago I knew a fine woman who had been within the Church all her life. Her husband was an office holder. To give open expression to her doubts might, she felt, threaten their marriage. So she stifled all the details until one day in a group meeting at the church she could contain herself no longer. Out it all came in a torrent of words accompanied by strong feelings. To her amazement this openness did something within the group. Others shared their own thoughts and feelings in ways they had never done before. The strange thing was that both she and the others went home happier than they had been for a long time.

No, they had not abandoned their faith. They did not opt out of the Church. They did, however, seek a greater willingness to be allowed to truly be themselves. They were not going to conform to a stereotype of what a Christian and Church member should be like. In my own life experience, particularly as I have grown older, I have come to see that following Jesus is the supremely important thing. It is the life and teaching of Jesus that sets before me an ideal way of life to which I seek to aspire. Even when I fail, my very failure provides the raw material of my growth into greater maturity. Jesus does not supply us with a rule book which has an answer to every difficult situation and which immediately clears up our every doubt. He calls us to follow him in what is an exciting adventure. Faith and doubt are not opposites. They coexist together to facilitate a growing Christian life.

> *I pray that they may always be happy people, held together by their love of men and God, and sure of the Good News in all its richness because they know what they believe. I want them to know the secret of it all – God's secret – Jesus himself.*
> *(Colossians 2:2, NW, p. 190)*

> *For the goodness of God is the highest prayer that reaches down to our lowest needs. It awakens our soul and brings it to life, and makes it grow in grace and virtue.*
> *(RDL, Chapter 6)*

Hello God – it's me _____

Our practice of prayer is often related to our childhood habits. I recall my 90-year-old grandma coming to stay with us when I was a boy. My brother and I used to listen to her saying her prayers in the next room. She always ended with the same words – 'If I should die before I wake, I pray the Lord my soul to take.' I am sure that her simple prayers meant much to her.

However, it is possible to use forms of words (The Lord's Prayer is the classic example) and to fail to put ourselves into the mould we are using. Such prayers can actually be an excuse for praying! It can even persuade us that we have *said our prayers.*

Prayer is essentially simple. God is our Father and we can go to him as a loving father and be perfectly natural with him. But this does not mean taking just the *religious* side of ourselves to him; it means taking the whole of ourselves and showing this to God when we pray. So today in this your quiet time use all the aids we are giving you in these meditations. Let them sink in deeply and stimulate honest reflection, but at some point also say . . . *Hello God – it's me* . . . Just tell him how you feel. Pour out your worries, your anxiety, your frustrations, and also the good things . . . your gratitude and sense of well-being. Just be yourself with him.

When you have done this then slow everything down. Keep one single thought in your mind or one single word. Use this device to expel all other racing thoughts and ideas. Then say . . . *Master, speak, your servant heareth.* Now just listen and expect to hear him speaking to you in the deepest depths of your being. He most certainly will.

When we pray, we speak to God just as Jesus did; we say 'Father!' God himself makes us quite sure in our hearts that we are his children . . . as God's children we share his wealth as heirs along with Jesus.
(Romans 8:14-17, NW, p. 259)

And so it is proper for us, by nature and grace, to long and yearn with all our strength to know ourselves. For in this knowledge we shall truly and clearly know our God in fullness of joy.
(RDL, Chapter 46)

Does praying make any difference?

On the morning I was writing this piece, the BBC *Today* programme featured a news item in which it discussed a claim made by psychology researchers at a British University that those who pray and worship regularly have a better mental and physical health record than those who don't. Of course, this claim was disputed by other contributors, one of whom claimed that another project had shown that similar results were found among those who played bingo regularly! The real underlying reason was, the critics claimed, the feeling of community engendered among both churchgoers and bingo players.

It may be that this claim has some substance. Psychologists tell us that there is a deep level of the human mind which we all share. Some call it the *collective unconscious*. What it means is that in some mystical way we are all connected. Deep down there is a kind of underground pool or reservoir which we all tap into. So both at church and in the bingo hall a sense of togetherness is fostered which is life enhancing.

Christian teaching would want to put the same truth but at a much deeper level. We belong to the *body of Christ* and we believe in the *communion of saints*. For Christians this has an added dimension. Our fellowship is with one another but it also involves Jesus. Paul used the phrase to be *in Christ* around 163 times in his letters. This surely sheds light on the quality of our interconnectedness. It is also a pointer as to how prayer makes a difference. Because, as the Bible says, we are all *bound up in the bundle of life*; we have a channel we can use to bring something good into other people's lives.

When you are concerned prayerfully for the needs of others the principle of serendipity comes into operation. The benefit which comes to ourselves is a worthy by-product. Yes, praying, being quiet before God, and then expressing our concerns for others does make a difference both to their lives and to ours. After all, true prayer is not about getting what we want; it is about lining ourselves up with God's will and purpose, or, to put it another way, to possess *the mind of Christ*. (See the opening piece on *Suggestions for the use of this devotional guide*.)

I go on living my ordinary life; and yet in a sense, I don't feel that I'm living it, but that Jesus has taken charge of me; I live by trusting in Jesus, God's Son, who loved me and gave his life for me.
(Galatians 2:20, NW, p. 304)

For if I look at myself alone, I am nothing. But when I think of myself and my fellow Christians joined together by love, I have hope. For in this joining lies the life of all who shall be saved.
(RDL, Chapter 9)

How to keep warm in winter _____

During a particularly cold spell in the depths of winter I put the above title for my sermon on a poster outside my church. It caused quite a stir. That was fifty years ago! However, I can still remember at least two of the points which I made to open up the theme. The first was *keep near the fire*. There was very little central heating in homes in those far-off days. The open coal fire was the order of the day and, when it was very cold, you certainly had to keep near to it if you wanted to keep warm.

Fire is a word associated with the gift of the Holy Spirit. On that wonderful Day of Pentecost there were signs and wonders and one of those signs is described as being like *tongues of fire*. The relevant question for us today is how do we maintain the spiritual glow? I was once in the company of an 80-year-old man and an 18-year-old girl at a midweek meditation in a Roman Catholic community. Both were talking about the new ways of praying to which they had been introduced. At one point the 80-year-old told the 18-year-old about how he envied her. He just wished he could have made the discovery many years ago.

The second point I made was *keep on the move*. Under this second heading I shared the importance of seeing life as a pilgrimage. My mind goes back to a group of middle-aged Christians who were sharing themselves at a deep level. Several of them spoke of the ways in which they had been influenced as teenagers but that now they had moved on. The original spark was still there but to keep it alive they had wrestled with perplexities and disappointments and now these had been incorporated into their pilgrimage. They had grown through their mental and emotional trials and tribulations and had kept on the move.

I am getting on in years, being well past my *sell-by date*, but I still want to keep moving on and making new discoveries. This is one of the exciting things about the Bible. You can read a familiar passage and then suddenly it happens. You are seeing things differently – in a new light. That is what we call inspiration!

> *Don't try to do what everybody does. Let God keep your mind alive and ready to think new thoughts, and you'll be a very different person from what you were. In this way you will be able to find what God wants you to be and to do – what is worthwhile and grown up.*
> *(Romans 12:2, NW, p. 274)*

> *In all this he takes the part of a kind nurse who has no other care but the welfare of her child. It is his office to save us, it is his glory to do it, and it is his will that we should know it. . . . For it is his will that we should love him dearly and trust him humbly and strongly. And he showed me this in these gracious words: 'I will hold you securely.'*
> *(RDL, Chapter 61)*

Vision

Paul saw a vision and heard a voice on the road to Damascus. That event transformed his life. Previously he was Saul; now he was Paul, friend of Jesus and apostle. Do people still have visions and hear voices? When I was coming to the end of my theological training I was eagerly awaiting news of my first appointment. When the news came I was disappointed. I was to be Minister/Warden of Preston Clubland. Now I felt that my primary calling was to be a preacher and here I was being designated as a youth club leader. On my way to Preston on a preliminary visit I had two hours to wait on Chester station. I wandered into the Cathedral. It was the only time I have ever been inside that holy place although now I live within 25 miles of that ancient city. I sat down in a pew in a corner. Tourists were milling around but I was alone. Suddenly I felt a quiet assurance deep within. Then an inner voice seemed to say, 'Don't worry, you will be all right.' That was all . . . but it was enough.

Soon after I was established in the job one of my senior members asked to see me. He was a young married man who worked in the building trade as a bricklayer. He had a cutting in his hand from our denominational newspaper. It was an advertisement for a Clerk of Works to oversee the building of a school in Chipembi in what was then Northern Rhodesia. Rather nervously he enquired if I thought he could do the job because he felt that God was saying something to him about his future and would this be the answer? I confess that I was doubtful. This was a managerial role and although I knew he was a good tradesman I wondered about his man-management skills, especially within a different culture. But that inner voice spoke to me again. 'Tell him to go for it!' I did. He went. When the school was built he went into the South African ministry and eventually came back to the UK as a brother Minister. Now, like me, he is retired after a lifetime of splendid service.

Yes, people do still have visions. God still speaks to people today. Find a disciplined quietness within yourself. Listen. Check out with a close friend and confidant what you have felt and heard. Then go for it!

God's answer to Jeremiah's reluctance was . . . 'You shall go to whomsoever I send you! You shall speak whatever I tell you! Don't be afraid of anybody – I am with you, I am looking after you.' (Jeremiah 1:7-8, WQ, p. 261)

If there is a lover of God anywhere on earth who is always kept safe from falling, I know nothing of it – for it was not shown me. But this is shown – that in falling and rising again we are always held close in one love. (RDL, Chapter 82)

Who am I?

The German martyr theologian Dietrich Bonhoeffer wrote a poem with this title just before he died on Adolf Hitler's orders immediately prior to the end of the Second World War. In it he explored the different aspects of his being which often seemed to be in conflict with each other. In the end, however, he reaches a major conclusion which he expresses in these words: *Whoever I am thou knowest O God, I am thine.* St Paul passed through a similar experience which he records in the Epistle to the Romans. *What an unhappy man I am*, he declares, but then goes on to thank God for delivering him from that constant inner struggle by enabling him *to live in union with Christ Jesus.*

A currently popular way of exploring this dilemma is to ask the question: Am I what I am through nature or through nurture? We know a great deal about our inherited genes which play their part in programming our individual lives. Our forebears pass on to us various physical, mental and emotional characteristics. Then the kind of stable love we receive brings us into the realm of nurture. If we are helped to feel safe and secure by our close bonding to our parents we are laying the foundations for a healthy growth into maturity.

All this is well-established. The study of human development has opened windows of understanding into how we become the people we are. There is, however, another factor which sadly not everyone takes into account. It is what we Christians call *grace*. This has been defined as *God's love in action.* When we come to God expressing our deeply felt needs then grace begins to function. The fact that we matter to God and that Jesus came to live and die to reveal this truth, this is the third factor – and it can make all the difference.

To introduce grace into our own human situations requires us to recognise that we have needs which can be freely expressed. Grace Sheppard, the wife of the former Bishop of Liverpool, is an agoraphobic. She fears wide open spaces. This feature of her personality was crippling her life. For years she told as few people as she needed to about her secret. One day she realised her mistake. She must be open about her need and she must seek help – both from God and from other understanding people. The result was a book which has helped thousands in seeking relief from their own inner conflicts. Its title? *In Place of Fear*. Now both nature and nurture have been complemented by grace – and this has made all the difference. The woman Grace has discovered God's grace as an experience.

It doesn't matter now what happens. I can face plenty and poverty. I can enjoy wealth and want. I've learned God's secret. There isn't anything I can't face: but I know where my strength comes from – it comes from Jesus.
(Philippians 4:11-13, NW, p. 190)

For all our life goes by threes: first we have our being, second we have our growing and third we have our fulfilment. The first is nature, the second is mercy, the third is grace.
(RDL, Chapter 58)

Honest to God

Ruth was a friend who died when she was only in her forties. She belonged to a religious community and specialised in working with children. She lived with bone cancer for four years and was correcting the proofs of a book she had written about children's prayers on the very day she died. During her illness she spoke about her love of the Psalms but not only because of the many expressions of confidence and comfort they contain. She loved the Psalms because from time to time the Psalmist railed against God in anger and misery. This was how she felt at times and the Psalmist provided her with both the words and the permission to be angry with God and to express her deep disappointments. After she had expressed her anger then she felt better and could move on to be more confident and trusting.

Gerald, another friend, died in his early fifties. He was a man who had passed through many tough times including the awful experience of being rejected. After his death I read an article he had written with the strange title, 'Too nice for words'. He wrote about the dangers of always trying to be seen as a nice person. In so doing we tend to cover up the real person who is hiding behind a mask. He acknowledged that there were aspects of his own personality that he did not like. Better to recognise this and acknowledge it in our dealings with God.

This also works out in our dealings with other people. I have known marriages that are held on to for the sake of respectability when the ability to communicate with one another has been totally absent. All honesty and openness has disappeared from their relationship. They stay together but life is a mutual misery. Such marriages can be saved if those involved can be helped to communicate better. I recall one such marriage I was trying to help with many years ago. In the course of our conversations

I said to the husband in his wife's presence, 'But you do love your wife, don't you?' His reply was terse but to the point, 'Of course I do.' This brought the wife into action and her acid comment was, 'That is the first time I have heard you say that in thirty years.' Things did begin to improve after this although it was a long, hard road.

Being honest with God requires us also to be honest with ourselves. The darker, negative aspects of our lives are more easily dealt with when they are recognised and acknowledged. Why not try to experiment with the idea of being more *honest to God*.

Rise up, O God! Why are you sleeping? Awake! Don't abandon us for ever. Why do you hide your face? Why take no notice of our distress? . . . Rise up! Come to our help! Rescue us in your steadfast love!
(Psalm 44:23-26, WQ, p. 398)

For this passing life does not ask that we live completely without blame and sin. He loves us endlessly, and we sin continually, and he shows us our sin most tenderly. And then we sorrow and mourn with discretion and turn to look upon his mercy, clinging to his love and goodness, knowing that he is our medicine . . .
(RDL, Chapter 82)

A comfortable rut

I was once inviting one of my Church members to become involved in an interesting, and indeed exciting, piece of work. He failed to respond positively and in his explanation he said, 'You see, I don't like to be disturbed. I'm in a very comfortable rut.'

It was hard to tell him how I felt but I feared for him. He had gifts and talents that could have been used in this useful area of Christian service. He was in grave danger of fossilisation!

Comfortable ruts are a temptation that comes to all of us at some time or other in our lives. This is particularly true about our personal relationship with God. We can so easily come to rely on the comfort and friendliness of our Church life, for instance. Messages from God flow over us so easily because we say to ourselves that we have heard it all before and we are quite safe anyway. We are on good terms with God.

I once belonged to a group which included a churchwarden at his local parish church. He told us that his daughter had asked him what it meant to come alive in the Holy Spirit. In reply he suggested that she take her question to the Vicar. She did but at the same time pursued the matter with her father. He started to go with her to a group meeting and met God in a new way. He didn't deny all his previous experience but admitted that it had all become routine and matter of fact. He didn't express it in this way but he was in a very comfortable rut. When he came out of it and began to relate his faith more radically to his lifestyle he came to life and this was the graphic way he described his transformation, 'I felt that I was lifted out of the Church's filing system'.

There are possibilities and opportunities that come to us *through all the changing scenes of life*. Through facing up to them we grow and develop – and we rise up out of our comfortable ruts.

This is why when the time was ripe, God sent his Son to live amongst us – to help us to live as his sons and daughters, grown-up members of his family. Because this is what we now are he has given us the Spirit of his Son in our hearts.
(Galatians 4:4-6, NW, p. 268)

And in his goodness he opens the eye of our understanding and gives us sight – sometimes more, sometimes less, as God makes us able to understand it.
(RDL, Chapter 52)

Touched by a loving hand

The title for this piece comes from an old hymn not sung very much these days. This is the whole verse:

> Touched by a loving hand,
> wakened by kindness,
> cords that were broken
> will vibrate once more.

Years ago I used to visit a Roman Catholic nun who was a patient in a hospital where I was one of the chaplaincy team. She was seriously ill and coming to the end of her earthly life. Each time after I had prayed with her she would beckon me to kneel by her bed. When I did so she placed her thin hand on my head and prayed for me. What I recall most of all was the power which flowed to me from her gentle touch. I just felt the presence of God coming into the deepest part of my being. Since that experience I have had an ever-increasing belief in the power of touch.

I recall reading about a man who woke one morning with a terribly stiff neck. Fortunately his physiotherapist daughter was staying with him and she began to massage and manipulate. When she had located a locked joint she pressed harder but the harder she pressed the more he resisted. He was in fact quite frightened by the intensity of her pressure. Her instruction to him to relax made no difference. Eventually she put a bag of frozen peas on the spot to ease the pain and left him. He then thought over what had happened and deliberately began some planned relaxation exercises. When she came back the same treatment she had offered before was given again – and this time it worked!

The healing power of touch from a loving person requires our co-operation. As we *rest in the Lord* so he comes to us in a special way. So here you are, just you and God. You want him to touch you as Jesus touched so many people in the days of his flesh. Use your imagination. Build up a picture of Jesus in your mind. Let all your tension and anxiety go. Get rid of disturbing thoughts by reminding yourself that you are accepted; that you are loved. Feel his hand resting upon you. Open your deepest self to his loving touch. The critics may talk about auto-suggestion. This may well be a channel which God uses. What does it matter? God is with you. His Son Jesus is touching you. Open up your needs to him. Relax. In the stillness *let God be God*. Then the cords that were broken *will vibrate once more*.

> *Believe me, the time is soon coming – in fact it is here now – when people who are living 'half dead' lives will hear the voice of the Son of God, and all who listen will learn the secret of being really alive. The Father is the source of all real life; he makes the Son the source of real life too.*
> *(John 5:25-26, NW, p. 313)*

> *And so I understand that every man or woman who chooses God of his own will in this life, for love, may be sure that he himself is loved without end. And this love gives him grace.*
> *(RDL, Chapter 65)*

Salvation

Salvation is a religious word which has at its root the idea of finding a more spacious existence. Its origins lie in the Old Testament conception of the chosen people of God – the Jews – being saved out of bondage in Egypt and being guided to move into a more spacious promised land. It began therefore with very practical consequences. A people who had been oppressed stood in need of an act of rescue. God came to their aid and the rescue event took place.

Throughout the New Testament, through the work and activity of Jesus, different people – the blind, the deaf, the disabled, the outcasts – were rescued from their former positions and given a new kind of dignity. Yes, there was deep spiritual meaning in what Jesus did for them but there were also practical consequences. They were better able to take their place in society because of what Jesus had done. 'For us men and for our salvation' meant not only a spiritual blessing; it was also a practical experience – they could see, hear, speak and walk!

All too often we have spiritualised the experience of personal salvation and have not laced the challenge to be saved with direct statements about the consequences. The rich evangelists who are driven about in huge cars and who live in splendid hotels may count up the decisions made and the numbers of people being saved but if their own lifestyle is badly in need of being rescued from itself, do they not deny the very gospel which they preach?

So the word *salvation* needs itself to be rescued from being presented as a narrow spiritual experience. To be rescued from a life of sin and rebellion against God means at one and the same time to be *saved* into a life of compassion and active love. Christian Aid, CAFOD, Tear Fund are all direct evidence of the greater spaciousness of the saved life. We need many more.

Remember who you are. God has chosen you, you belong to him and he loves you. His way must be your way. Care for people. Be kind and gentle and never think about yourself. Stand up to everything. Put up with people's wounding ways; when you have real cause to complain, don't – forgive them.
(Colossians 3:12-13, NW, p. 290)

A cheerful giver does not count the cost of what he gives. His heart is set on pleasing him to whom the gift is given. And if he who receives it takes the gift with joyful thanks, the courteous giver thinks it has cost him nothing compared with the joy and happiness he has in pleasing and delighting the one he loves.
(RDL, Chapter 23)

I have been baptised

Many couples, be they married or living as partners, do not present their children for baptism today. However, some have felt the need for some kind of naming ceremony during which they affirm their love and loyalty towards the child. I respect this. I have never refused to baptise a child when requested but I was often unhappy about some who were presented to me. I always asked why the parents were making this request and the classic answer repeated in different forms was, 'Because we shall never get Gran to stop nagging us until we get him/her done!' Or sometimes it was Mum who nagged – but seldom Dad.

I was asked by my daughter and son-in-law to dedicate our first grandchild, Thomas. I did so willingly because they had thought their way through this and made a conscious decision. They also wrote the service themselves. Later, when Thomas was about 7, he began to ask questions about the baptisms he had seen taking place in the church to which they belonged. As a result he, even at that tender age, asked to be baptised. He was, and a most moving service took place in which he made his own responses. Thomas, now a thoughtful 18-year-old, does not attend church regularly but I was glad that he was baptised. He certainly shows the 'fruits of the Spirit' in his care of people and in his compassion for those in need.

I don't have a rigid theology of baptism. I am in favour of ecumenical situations when baptism is offered to young children on the basis of the faith of parents and the local Christian community but also offers a service of dedication to be followed by believer's baptism if and when that time arrives.

It was Martin Luther who, when in dark despair, flung his inkwell at the wall of his cell and cried out, 'I have been baptised'.

In so doing he was appealing to what he believed was an act of God's grace. He was continually seeking to fulfil what had been begun in his baptism. Like Luther I am glad that I have been baptised.

> *Philip told a high officer in the Queen of Egypt's administration about the good news of Jesus. As they were going along the road they came to some water. 'Look – there's water here,' said the officer, 'what's to stop me joining the friends of Jesus here and now?'... Philip baptised him there and then; and the officer joined the company of the friends of Jesus.*
> *(Acts 8:26-40, NW, p. 149)*

> *And he nourishes us with all the sweet sacraments, with full mercy and grace. And this is what he meant by that blessed word when he said: It is I that holy church preaches and teaches you (which) means this, 'All the healing and life of the sacraments, all the virtue and grace of my word, all the goodness that is set down by holy church for you – it is I'.*
> *(RDL, Chapter 60)*

The lonely road

He became a casual friend when I was a young minister. Then our paths divided but I watched his progress from a distance. I noted the appointments that came his way. I always felt that he would go far. He had good communication skills. He was a likeable character. Imagine my sadness when I heard that he had become an alcoholic. The consequences were heartbreaking. His marriage failed. He lost his high-powered job. He was out there on his own without friends and without hope.

Then something positive did happen. He had to go into hospital and whilst there was befriended by two young doctors. They helped him to take a long hard look at himself. Yes, he had sought success and he loved the limelight. Now all that was gone he felt that he had little to live for. These two young doctors reminded him of the Jesus he had sought to serve. He too faced a lonely road. He faced rejection but in the end he triumphed. My friend of long ago (call him Ray) began the long climb back and was given an appointment with good staff support. His one desire now was to be useful and to have a place in society which would give him a renewed hope.

I wrote to him after an interval of 35 years. He came to spend a Sunday with us in our manse. He told something of his story in the morning service in my church. It was real stuff born out of his bitter experiences. My congregation warmed to him.

After lunch my wife left us to talk. He described his high-powered job which had brought him into contact with peers, politicians, senior Churchmen and indeed royalty. 'You see, Howard,' he said, 'I knew everybody – but in reality I knew nobody. I was always good for a few drinks – but nobody seemed to care about the real me.'

End of story? Not quite. He was reunited with his wife and

family. He conquered his drink habit – and he died knowing that he was loved both by God and by some other people.

Might we today help someone to realise that they are wanted and loved? As my friends in The Grail Community put it: 'To help one person to grow is to help to build the world.'

> *If we are strong, our business is to help people who are weak. We have no right to 'please ourselves'. It's the fellow next to us we should 'please' – to help him to be himself and to grow up. Remember – Jesus never 'pleased himself'.*
> *(Romans 15:1-3, NW, p. 287)*

> *And so our good Lord answered all the doubts and questions I could raise, saying so comfortably: 'I am able to make all things well. I know how to make all things well, and I shall make all things well. And you shall see for yourself that all manner of things shall be well.'*
> *(RDL, Chapter 31)*

Accentuate the positive ⎯⎯⎯⎯⎯

As I write this piece the BBC is presenting a series of programmes designed to help viewers to kick the habits of smoking, excessive drinking and over-eating leading to obesity. I have been fortunate never to have acquired the smoking habit although I did experiment as a teenager. Alcohol equally has never been a problem because although I am not a tee-totaller I do not actually like the taste of beer or spirits. The odd glass of wine or cider represents the height of my alcoholic indulgence. But obesity has always been a problem. In spite of the excuses that I make for myself I know that my being over-weight is entirely my fault. The intake of calories has been greater than my human burn-up rate. However, my becoming a 'late onset diabetic' has actually been a health asset. My doctor said as much in a conversation with my wife: 'The best thing that could have happened to him,' was his expression. I am not sure about that but it is undoubtedly easier to control eating habits when the dangers of uncontrolled sugar diabetes are pointed out to you.

The words *discipline* and *disciple* come from the same root and are closely interlinked. Personal discipline is required of the disciples of Jesus Christ but there has been an unfortunate spin-off from this. The Christian faith is seen by some as call-ing for a negative approach to living based upon the *'thou shalt not'* emphasis in the Ten Commandments as detailed in Exo-dus 20. However, even the Old Testament commandments are not entirely negative and it is surely interesting to note that when the Old Testament commandments are superseded by the New Testament commandments the negative gives way entirely to the positive in the twin emphasis upon love of God and love of neighbour (Matthew 22:27-30).

I do not recall which psychologist it was who coined the

phrase *the expulsive power of a new affection* but I have seen such a concept in action on numerous occasions. A fellow student used to wander around the college corridors with scarcely ever a smile and a kind of mild depression seemed to colour all of his activities. Then one summer he fell in love and when he came back for the Autumn term he was transformed. I have seen personal slimming campaigns succeeding against all odds because the person concerned wanted to become more beautiful and acceptable to a potential admirer.

The discipline that goes hand in hand with Christian discipleship can be creative and fruitful when it is inspired by love.

I am quite sure that nothing – neither dying nor living, neither what we are facing now nor what we may have to face tomorrow, nothing in our own world or in outer space or in our own hearts, can take away from us God's love, made real by Jesus our Lord.
(Romans 8:38-39, NW, p. 261)

And from this it comes that there is nothing, and shall be nothing, between God and man's soul. And in this endless love man's soul is kept whole. And in this endless love we are led and looked after by God, and shall never be lost.
(RDL, Chapter 53)

Journey into space —————————————

Journeys into space have become almost everyday events. That one small step down on to the surface of the moon was a giant leap in scientific achievement and said much for human courage and the spirit of adventure. The cost was enormous but the consequences have not as yet done much to improve the lives of ordinary men and women down here on earth.

But there is another kind of journey into space that can make a profound difference to human happiness and wellbeing. This is the adventurous journey into our own inner space. How is this achieved? First of all there must be a desire to discover more about ourselves. We know that we are fearfully and wonderfully made and this not only applies to our well-designed and ordered physical qualities. It also applies to the mind and the heart. Deep down within us is *the still point of the turning world.*

We call this our soul. It is where motivations and desires are to be discovered. It is where we get to know the kind of people we really are. I have found this journey both challenging and disturbing. This past week I found myself feeling uncomfortable as I sought my inner space. There I found the green-eyed monsters of envy and jealousy. How did I cope? First of all by recognising them and accepting them for what they are. The negative side of my life is real. It is like a caged beast anxious to break out and do damage. By naming it I take the first step to disarming it. Then I try to accentuate the positive. I take a look at Jesus and remind myself that I am loved. This tends to minimise the effects of the negative.

Old choruses have a way of coming into the mind at exactly the right time. Sometimes a little sentimental perhaps, but refreshing and helpful just the same. This is the chorus that helped me this week:

Turn your eyes upon Jesus, look full in his wonderful face,
and the things of earth will grow strangely dim,
in the light of his glory and grace.

I haven't got anywhere near being the kind of man I want to be; and I haven't become as mature as Jesus was – by a long way. But nothing's going to stop me now, I intend to be the kind of person Jesus wanted me to be when he called me on the Damascus Road. (Philippians 3:12-16, NW, p. 199)

And sometimes when our hearts are dry and cannot feel, or when we are surrounded by temptation, then we are driven by reason and by grace to call upon our Lord with our voice, recalling his blessed Passion and great goodness. (RDL, Chapter 41)

Helpful people

As I look back over my life I think, from time to time, of the people who have helped me. They are legion and many of them don't know me and I don't know them. These are the ones who have helped me through books, sermons and broadcasts. But for the ones that I do remember, what have been the reasons why I believe that they have helped me at some stage in my life?

1. *They valued me.* At an early stage in my life I lacked confidence. I did not value myself. These people had faith in me and so enabled me to have faith in myself. They wrote letters to me and gave me books to read.

2. *They listened to me.* They sat back and gave me their undivided attention. If it seemed right they shared themselves with me. Then they helped me work things out for myself and didn't try to pressurise me.

3. *They encouraged me.* This was especially helpful in assisting me to realise my strengths. The fact that I had gifts and abilities through which other people could find help was a revelation to me.

4. *They prayed for me.* What did this mean? Not so much keeping my name on a list and repeating it from time to time in a mechanical way, but seeing me in healthy and creative ways; putting me in God's presence; using their imagination to let Jesus touch me.

Occasionally I get telephone calls and written messages from right out of the blue. I do not know the people concerned or I have forgotten all about them. But they contact me to tell me that something I have written or said, spoke to them and helped them to move on to a new stage in life. Such experiences always give me a real thrill. It is good to be used by God.

You could be today – by valuing others; listening to their expressions of need; encouraging them – and praying for them.

My dear friends, let us really care for one another; such care and love is God's gift to us. Everybody who loves and cares is his son or daughter, and knows God. Those who have no love in their hearts for anybody haven't the slightest idea what God is like, for the very heart of God is love.
(1 John 4:7-12, NW, p. 298)

And grace works – raising up, rewarding and end-lessly outstripping all that our loving and our labour deserve – spreading abroad and showing the high, huge wholeness of God's royal lordship, in his won-derful courtesy. And this is the abundance of love.
(RDL, Chapter 48)

Creation and creativity _____

'In the beginning – God', this is the basic affirmation of faith. God is before anything else. Spirit is prior to matter. What follows from this? Surely the truth that God is in the world we inhabit and an integral part of it. He did not wind up the world like a clock and then depart. God is love. He showed this in Jesus and then gave us the Holy Spirit to constantly remind us that Jesus is alive today.

God's purpose for us now is that we should be at home in our Father's house – make the most of it, enjoy it. Share what you enjoy. Co-operate with God in caring for each other and for our environment. Whatever our political persuasion we should all have green aspirations.

There is a fascinating and challenging consequence to this our own life of faith. Paul sums this up for us in Ephesians 2:10: 'We are his workmanship, created in Christ Jesus unto good works.' This surely means that we have the inestimable privilege of sharing in his ongoing creation. My own experience both as a disciple of Jesus Christ and as a working pastor made me realise that we are often capable of exerting a greater influence than we give ourselves credit for.

When I began my ministry I spoke regularly in the open air. Every Sunday evening after service would see me in the market square standing on a box and sharing the good news, mainly by the question and answer method. It was a good argument that brought the crowds. But after a time I needed a rest; a short break so that my voice could be restored in strength. I spoke first to one young woman who had recently become a Christian. I asked her if she would just take my place on the box and tell her own personal story. Hesitantly she agreed. When it happened for the first time the crowd listened in silence. There was no heckling. What a difference it made to her own faith – and what an impression her simple sharing had upon the listeners. More than one person began their personal preaching ministries in that open air meeting.

Ask God to show you those as yet undiscovered gifts by which you can more actively share in his ongoing creation.

In the beginning of all things – the Word. God and the Word, God himself . . . The Word became human and lived a human life like ours. We saw his splendour, love's splendour, real splendour. . . . From the richness of his life all of us have received endless kindness.
(John 1:1-18, NW, pp. 300-301)

And this is how every soul should think inwardly of its lover: that is to say the love of God makes such a bond between us that, when this is seen truly, no man can separate himself one from another. And this is why our soul ought to think that God has done all that he has done for him alone.
(RDL, Chapter 65)

Righteous anger

Coral Atkins was an actress who starred in a successful TV series entitled *Family at War*. Her life was changed by a chance encounter with a child in the care of the local authority in a home for especially difficult children. She was angry with what she saw as a form of detached care which lacked human warmth and love. She decided to establish a home of her own for such children where real family love would be the prevailing factor. Then began a long struggle with the child care professional authorities who did everything they could to prevent her realising her dream. The driving force behind her eventual success was her deep-seated anger at what she saw as totally unsuitable forms of care. Eventually it emerged that during wartime evacuation she and her sister had been subjected to abuse and cruelty. This emerged during her sessions with a sympathetic psychiatrist who had backed her efforts but who recognised that the anger drive had to be understood and controlled if she was to achieve lasting success. Later in life Coral Atkins became a lay psychotherapist and was able to continue her pioneering efforts with the added advantage of being able to reflect more positively upon her own inner turbulence. But it was her anger that originally empowered her to succeed in helping many children to discover happiness.

Do you sometimes fear that your own personal anger could be destructive to your own growth and development as a Christian pilgrim?

Do you remember what happened to Jesus when he was faced with the scenes of graft and corruption inside the Holy Temple, the House of God? Some might say that Jesus *lost it* and hit out in uncontrolled anger even to the extent of using a whip and physically tipping over the tables of the money changers, presumably scattering their ill-gotten gains! Surely it is nearer the truth to say that Jesus *found it* because his anger was not just blind and destructive; it was righteous anger and it was controlled by love. What he saw was an affront to God and humanity. So he cleansed the temple.

The Salvation Army's founder, William Booth, was angry at the plight of the poor in darkest London. Dr Barnardo was angry at the condition of the street children of his day who slept in cardboard boxes. Out of anger came good. This was because that anger was controlled by love. The end result was both positive and creative.

Where love is denied, let love break through – sometimes because I'm angry!

> *You have searched the depth of my being, O God, you know all about me – when I'm resting, when I'm working. You have probed my deepest intentions, tracking out the road I take, and my camping ground. You know me through and through. Understanding better than I what I'm trying to say.*
> *(Psalm 139:1-4, WQ, p. 402)*

> *In all this he takes the part of a kind nurse who has no other care but the welfare of her child. It is his office to save us, it is his glory to do it, and it is his will that we should know it. ... And he showed this in these gracious words: 'I will hold you securely.'*
> *(RDL, Chapter 61)*

Faith and health

My old friend Dr Michael Wilson died recently. He was both priest and doctor. In his final illness he exemplified what he had written and spoken about what health really is all about. He recognised that there could be health within physical weakness – as I am quite sure there was in his own case. He related faith and health as is shown in his thoughtful definition: *Health is the ability to respond in a mature way to life as it is.*

1. *Faith gives life meaning.* Dr Victor Frankl wrote two books about his experiences as a prisoner in Hitler's concentration camps. He observed that those who had some sort of faith seemed to hold together better under terrible strain. Faith for them was a cohesive factor enabling their survival. The title of one of those books is significant. It is *Man's Search for Meaning.*

2. *Faith enables our development and growth as disciples and thus as persons.* There are three potentially destructive areas of life which true faith can deal with, albeit often slowly and in stages. They are the inability to handle conflict; being unable to cope with failure and being overwhelmed by past experience. All these three I have come up against at different times in my life. At such times it is tempting to dive into our favourite 'bolt holes' such as only meeting with people who think like we do. As I had to discover, challenges relating to past hurts and past inadequacies have to be faced and conquered. This is what God's grace is all about.

3. *Faith provides goals to work towards.* To have goals to work towards at various stages in our lives is a healthy, life-enhancing process. Our main goal is surely to realise the Kingdom of God both in our own personal lives and in the communities of which we are a part.

4. *Faith facilitates a proper confidence.* Terry Waite was undoubtedly a man of honour and integrity but his faith took a bat-
   tering from time to time. This meant that he joined the
   Psalmist and the Patriarch Job now and then in expressing
   his true feelings to God – even when those feelings were of
   doubt and anger. He always felt better (i.e. more healthy)
   when he had found release in this way. I endorse this.

Yes, there is a link between faith and health.

> *And I'm tough with my body; I let it know who's master.*
> *After spending my life training others, I'm not going*
> *to be left at the post myself.*
> *(1 Corinthians 9:24-27, NW, p. 278)*

> *We shall gain lowliness and humbleness from looking*
> *on our own failure – and because of this we shall be*
> *raised high in heaven. And we could never have reached*
> *such height without such humbling.*
> *(RDL, Chapter 61)*

Treating raised blood pressure ___

When I was being medically examined as a candidate for the ministry of the Methodist Church I was told that my blood pressure was too high for the young man I then was. I was referred to my own doctor who told me that my blood pressure was normal. Later on in the mid-stream of my ministry my doctor told me that my blood pressure was too high and recommended medication. I have taken some medication ever since but the amount has been reduced to an absolute minimum. During this time I have been helped to see that when my emotional anxiety has been high and I have been unsettled within, this has affected my physical state of which increased blood pressure is an indicator. The ability to discover and maintain an inner quiet has become an essential part of my personal discipline.

A leading consultant physician came to address us one year in the Churches Council of Health and Healing. He told us about one of his suggested treatments for those who had come to him because of heart attacks or strokes or because their own Doctors thought that they were in danger of such conditions. In addition to the usual medical prescriptions he invited them to consider a revision of their personal lifestyles. One way to do this, he advocated, was to go away and spend time in a Retreat House. Those who accepted this advice seemed to do better than those who didn't.

The emphasis upon spiritual care within the modern National Health Service may not indicate a religious revival but it does indicate that for men and women to become more whole people, attention must be paid to the spiritual dimension.

There is abundant evidence that a consumer-orientated society in which the emphasis is upon acquiring more material possessions creates an unhealthy environment for a more natural growth into becoming fully human persons. One of Charles Causley's poems speaks about bringing the living to life. If this does follow from the divine-human encounter then one of the direct consequences may be less beta-blocker prescriptions for raised blood pressure!

> The Spirit is the source of real life; human nature by itself gets nowhere. My words – all I have said to you – are full of God's power and they are the secret of real life.
> (John 6:63, NW, p. 315)

> We must cling to God reverently and trust in him only. For God sees things one way and man sees them in another. For it falls to man to accuse himself humbly, and it falls to God, in his own true goodness, to excuse man courteously.
> (RDL, Chapter 52)

The wounded healer

A friend of mine who entered the ministry rather later in life than most of us received a letter from someone he had learned to love and trust just as he was about to be ordained. This is what the letter said: 'I feel that I am part of your ministry from the first day long ago when you indicated some inkling of a call. … At the risk of preaching to you can I quote to you some words from Henri Nouwen: "Like Jesus, he who proclaims liberation is called not only to care for his own wounds and the wounds of others, but also to make his own wounds the source of healing power."'

Mother Julian, who is helping us each day in these readings, coined a wonderful sentence when she wrote: *Our wounds can become our worships.* Early one morning just after I had read these words I felt moved to write a hymn. Here it is:

> His wounds are healing wounds,
> which show his love for me:
> they penetrate my inward heart,
> 'All this I did for thee.'
>
> My wounds are part of me,
> healed now, though scars remain;
> forgiven hurts enable me,
> reach others in their pain.
>
> Come, be my welcome guest,
> my heart is open wide;
> relive your hurts in confidence,
> the Lord is on your side.
>
> Then go your way in peace,
> your wounds and his combine;
> to progress your discipleship,
> and cause the sun to shine.

Long years ago a woman told me about some secret fears of what she might do to a loved one. I was able to tell her that I had known similar fears but had won through. We cried together and found a mutual healing experience.

> *The love of Jesus drives us on – when we realise that he gave his life for all mankind, so that everybody should have something bigger to live for than just himself. Jesus gave his life for everybody. . . . We try to think of people as God thinks of them.*
> *(2 Corinthians 5:14-17, NW, p. 263)*

> *For a soul that looks on these things shall see when it is touched by grace, that the pains of Christ's passion go beyond all other pains and, true to tell, that these same pains shall be turned into endless joys through Christ's passion.*
> *(RDL, Chapter 20)*

A grief observed

This is the title of a book by the late C. S. Lewis. It tells the story of his own awful sense of loss when his wife Joy died after their all-too-brief marriage. As a working pastor I have held on to people many times during the devastating grief of bereavement. But there are other kinds of grief. You may well grieve at your own sense of failure in some area of your life. You will grieve when you are badly let down or when you let someone else down. You may grieve when a member of your family becomes involved in doubtful activities. The reasons for grief are many and varied.

The important thing is what happens *through* such an experience. The young son of a family in one of my churches was killed in an accident. He fell from the high wall of a ruined building and died instantly. It was a time of enormous grief and suffering for the rest of the family. One positive thing that eventually emerged was that I was able to put the parents in touch with *The League of Compassionate Friends.* This organisation was founded by parents who had passed through similar experiences. They had all lost a child either through illness or accident. In coming together with others who shared the same experience they found comfort and strength. I happened also to know one of the founders. She is a fine woman with deep inward reserves from her vital Christian faith. She also has organising skills which she has utilised in the creation of this now national (and indeed international) organisation. Her grief at the time of her own loss was enormous but she did not allow the experience to turn her inwards upon herself. She looked outwards to others and their needs – and with what beneficial results!

Grief of any kind must be expressed. It must be shared with others, especially those you can trust. Bereavement counselling is widely available and in many areas is linked with the hospice movement. I have known many casualties of grief over the years. They have thought it their duty to grieve inwardly and outwardly for the rest of their lives. They have become burdens to their family and indeed to society. Unexpressed grief can be the starter for various illnesses including depression. *A grief observed* does not mean a grief forgotten. It is a sad experience which has been lived through and woven into the tapestry of life – and through which others can be comforted and helped.

> *He gives new life to those who are worn out; he revives those who are ready to drop! Commandos get tied and faint, seasoned veterans fall out with fatigue; but those who trust God grow stronger and stronger – soaring like eagles, running without tiring, marching without flagging!*
> *(Isaiah 40:29-31, WQ, p. 287)*

> *Our failing is full of fear. Our falling is full of shame. And our dying is full of sorrow. But in all this, the sweet eye of pity and love never looks away from us, nor does the working of mercy ever cease.*
> *(RDL, Chapter 48)*

Unlock the door _____

Most people can recall the day when they were locked out of their own home. The door had closed behind you and your key was still in the house. What a relief when, by one means or another, the door was opened and you were able to gain access to your own home and possessions.

Faith in Jesus also unlocks doors. It enables better communication with yourself first and then with other people. Take saying you are sorry, for instance. Apologising. Admitting that you were in the wrong. Not easy, but when it is called for, abundantly worthwhile.

Years ago a man of senior years made a commitment to Christ in a Holy Week Mission. He knew immediately that he had to seek to heal a break with his eldest son with whom he was not on speaking terms. He went round to his home the following morning only to find his overtures rejected. His son would not listen to what had happened to his father.

A few weeks later that same son was on my doorstep with tears in his eyes. 'Dad has died suddenly,' he told me, 'and we were never reconciled. I will never forgive myself.'

I recall another related experience. One of my church officers was fiercely independent. His particular domain was entirely his own. Even I as the church's minister had to keep my finger out of his particular pie. I felt that it could not go on. The spiritual wellbeing of the whole church was being affected. But when I opened my heart to him, I was rejected. I was told that what I had tried to share was a figment of my own imagination. Sadly, the door remained tightly closed – locked, bolted and barred. We soldiered on without any resolution of the problem until he moved away. But in that particular area of church life they were wasted years.

Another similar incident was so different. I sensed unease between myself and another of my church officers and tackled him about it. 'You like your own way too much,' was his explanation, 'and you try to manipulate us to do just what you want. We have minds of our own, you know.' I realised that it was true. My enthusiasm had got the better of my judgement. I told him so – and there was a gracious response. We became the best of friends and I ministered to him when he was dying.

Unlock the doors – and the King of glory shall come in!

You have searched out the truth in the depth of my being; teach me wisdom in my secret heart. . . . Don't look at the wrong I've done, blot it all out!
(Psalm 51:6-9, WQ, p. 401)

[A profitable understanding] is the lowliness and humbleness we shall gain from looking on our failure – and because of this we shall be raised high in heaven. And we could never have reached such height without such humbling.
(RDL, Chapter 61)

The courage to be _____

One of the problems I had to face as a young minister was to live up to people's expectations of me. I had to be always available; always smiling; always in a good temper; always ready to respond positively to their every request. The trouble was I didn't always feel like smiling. I did not want to be always available. Their requests were sometimes irksome and often totally unnecessary. Sadly I didn't ever have the courage to tell them exactly how I was feeling. So I put on a false front. I tried to be the kind of person they wanted me to be. I failed to be myself and in the end this constant pressure edged me towards a mini-breakdown.

At about the same time that I was feeling these pressures a woman of senior years, deeply respected by all who knew her, came to me in great distress. She and her husband had never been blessed with children but she had taken into her home another woman, slightly older than herself, when she had no home to go to. She was a person of some means and had paid her way adequately. Over the years that action had been regretted and a deep resentment of this invasion of their privacy had built up. She had never expressed it and even her husband was not aware of it. Now, during Holy Week, this had come to the surface. She went straight home and told her friend just how she had been feeling. The friend surprised her by saying that deep down she had known this for a long time – and also she understood. She would be quite happy to move into a residential home.

But there was no need. Once this festering sore had been revealed it seemed to disappear. Their friendship was reborn now on a much deeper level. They then both wished that the hurt had been exposed earlier.

Do you need to discover the inner resources to be more honest and open at least with some people? Do you really want the courage to be?

> *God's way . . . has everything to do with (a) putting wrong things right, (b) learning to live together as friends, and enjoying being alive because you know in your hearts that God is Father. Anybody who 'follows Jesus' by living like this is the sort of person God wants him to be – and his fellow men respect him too.*
> *(Romans 15:16-19, NW, p. 286)*

> *There is such an amazing mixture in us that we scarcely know how we or our fellow Christians stand because of these astonishing mixed feelings. But the same holy will, which we give to God when we perceive him, is always truly willing us to be with him – with all our heart and strength.*
> *(RDL, Chapter 52)*

Religious myopia

This is a condition in which there is a lack of clarity in vision. The old saying about the baby and the bath water applies here. The life of Christian discipleship is usually set within the context of the institutional Church. No one knows this better than someone like me – a professionally religious person. I have often been so caught up in the world of church organisation and even church politics that I have tended to forget what it is all about.

I sometimes shock some of my friends by gently suggesting that we are in danger of becoming too religious. My own simple theology suggests to me that Jesus was not concerned to be at the heart of a religious system. He was concerned to show people how to live and how to love. He himself lived life *in depth* but he was not always consciously being religious. He enjoyed meeting people and really caring for them.

Oh yes, I know that some kind of institutional Christianity is necessary and that if we got rid of one kind we would have to formulate another. The tragedy is that our religious systems with their individual peculiarities such as who can properly meet together for Holy Communion at the Lord's Table and what is or is not the right mode of Holy Baptism – these have become barriers not just between Christians but between churchgoing Christians and the secular society in which we operate. People realise their need of some form of inward spirituality. They are attracted by the person of Jesus but they are put off by the attitude of so many of the Jesus people to one another.

Here in the words of Thomas Merton is the challenge I would like to put to whosoever will on behalf of Jesus:

'The encounter with Christ liberates something in us, a power we did not know we had; a hope, a capacity for life, a resilience, an ability to bounce back when we thought we were completely defeated; a capacity to grow, and change; a power of creative transformation.'[1]

The major truth is that in following Christ in naked simplicity we look at life through a new pair of spectacles which delivers us from religious myopia.

You've heard people [saying] 'Our religion's the right religion; other people are just superstitious; we're civilised; they're wogs . . .' We don't talk like this any more. We stand – always and everywhere – for all that Jesus stood for. Jesus has broken down all barriers. He is all that matters and he is changing the whole life of mankind.
(Colossians 3:5-11, NW, p. 263)

He fires our understanding, he directs our ways, he comforts our soul. . . . And he makes us love all that he loves, for love of him, and to be well satisfied by him and all his works. (RDL, Chapter 61)

1 Thomas Merton in *He Is Risen.*

First Communion _____

This is a unique experience for some people. Our Roman Catholic friends prepare their young people at an early age and taking their first communion is a very special occasion – marked with festive clothing and feasting. I cannot remember my own first communion but I can remember the first time I celebrated Holy Communion. I was not ordained but I was a probationer minister and I had a written dispensation from the President of the Methodist Conference to preside at communion services. It was a midweek service in West Auckland Methodist Church and my first visit. When I arrived I was told that those responsible for preparation had run out of communion wine. Bread was available but no wine. Would we have to cancel the service?

Now I had anticipated this occasion with considerable expectation. I recall remembering that Jesus had changed water into wine and it seemed to me that here was my canonical authority to celebrate Holy Communion with water and bread. I did not expect the water to be changed into wine but I did expect the faith of the recipients – including me – to be of such a nature that it would be a real communion. It most certainly was!

Since then I have conducted thousands of communion services. I often say to myself and to those invited to the Holy Table that at least two things are necessary. They are that *we all need to repent and we all need to cultivate the ability to receive.*

When we come to communion we need to come repenting. I usually give communicants time to make personal confession in silence. It is in itself a healthy exercise.

A woman I knew well years ago was generous in hospitality – but sadly she found it most difficult to receive hospitality from other people – including us. This prevented our relationship from growing deep and meaningful. When we come to communion we come with open hands. Into those hands are placed *the dear tokens of his passion*; those sacred symbols so rich in meaning and significance. How important to take them right into the centre of our beings.

When I was a teenager I used to sing a simple chorus: *'Into my heart; into my heart, come into my heart, Lord Jesus. Come in today, come in to stay, come into my heart, Lord Jesus.'* I often say those words to myself when kneeling at the Holy Table.

Jesus, by his death, made us God's friends – even though we were then God's enemies. Now we are God's friends, Jesus, living in our hearts, can all the more deliver us from what is evil and help us to live as God created us to live.
(Romans 5:6-11, NW, p. 259)

For this is the spiritual thirst of Christ – a love-longing to have us all gathered together and made whole in him to his great joy, as I see it. For we are not now as wholly joined to him as we shall be then.
(RDL, Chapter 31)

Please pray for me _____

I was listening to my wife's side of a telephone conversation. I heard her say, 'I do every day and I will now.' I knew that she was responding to a direct request for prayer. I write this piece early on a Sunday morning. Later I shall be leading morning worship and I know that I shall be given the names of members of the congregation to include in the intercessory prayers. Does it make any difference? This is the question I often ask myself and it is one I have been frequently asked by other people.

I believe that it does but it is a rather different process from shopping in, say, a village store. Here we know what we want; we pay the recognised price and we get exactly what we ask for. It is when this kind of thinking is transferred to the nature of the prayer relationship with God that we get into trouble. We don't always get what we ask for. Sometimes it seems as if there is no answer at all. Sometimes the response from God's side is not what we expected or desired.

The idea of God who needs to be prayed to in order to change his mind about an individual just will not do. Some of those involved in prayer chains seem to encourage the idea that if we only get enough people involved God will do just what we ask. Happily – yes I did use that word – happily it doesn't work like that. Then how does it work?

God's love and mercy is always directed towards those about whom we are concerned. What we do when we pray specifically for them is to link in with those spiritual energies that come from God and are available to us all. We show solidarity with those for whom we pray. We flow out in love and compassion towards them. We are not trying to get God to change the way he functions in his own world. We are affirming that way and becoming part of it. We are giving life to the fact that at the deepest level of our inward selves we can be at one with God and with those for whom we pray. We are thus strengthening those channels and focusing both God's love and ours upon the one for whom we are praying.

We then leave the outcome in God's hands knowing that he can do abundantly more than we can ask or think. The simple truth is that in praying for those in special need we are not trying to change God's mind, we are seeking to become more and more adjusted to God's mind, for the outcome in the end can only be for the benefit of those who are at the heart of our prayers.

> *Think of building a house. The builders lay the foundations, use the stones to build the walls and hold them together with a keystone. . . . Jesus holds God's family together and helps it to grow, but he needs you, as the keystone needs the stones that make the walls. (Ephesians 2:19-22, NW, p. 289)*

> *But our good Lord the Holy Ghost, who is endless life living in our soul, looks after us safely. He puts peace in our soul and gives it ease, through grace. He attunes it to God and makes it willing. And this is the work of mercy, and the way our Lord continually leads us the whole time we are here in this changing life. (RDL, Chapter 48)*

The art of becoming

Human growth and development is a terrifying process. The embryonic child in the womb is safe and secure. Nourishment is constantly available and there is all-round protection. Then comes the moment of exit. First the waters break and then the contractions begin which eventually push the newly born child out into the big, scary world. The cord is cut but the bonding is not over, indeed it now reaches its most significant stage. Now the warmth of the breast and the mother's embrace become all important. Father also lends a supportive arm. Foundations are being laid.

Then one day the guiding hand is temporarily taken away. Other hands are available – grandparents, nursery school leaders – eventually teachers and young people's organisation leaders. But those who have given life through their own bonding still remain essential. Their mutual love; their constancy; their care; these are supremely important.

But other stages lie ahead. Bodily development brings strange and hitherto unknown feelings. We experiment; we make mistakes; we feel guilty yet often excited at future prospects. Sometimes we regress; we go backwards instead of forwards. The child within emerges in our cries for help as our inadequacies take over.

Then suddenly we realise that the process has come full circle. Now there are those who need us; who look to us for the kind of support we have usually received. This is terrifying in itself. Have I the necessary strength within myself? Have I known enough of love to be able to give love to others?

As I write I have just been handling a hymn book which my wife and I (then unmarried) gave to my father at Christmas 1944. Inside was an additional hymn sung at my mother's funeral – 'The old rugged cross'. Memories have been evoked. Feelings have emerged. Mixed feelings. Childhood was not always overwhelmingly happy. Yet I am grateful for the love I received.

Spiritual longings came early to me. I felt the need to discover a power from outside myself. My own childhood experiences, both positive and negative, helped me to try to understand my own children and to love them as they needed to be loved – and to eventually let them go into their own independent lives. In all this process to become aware that God loved me was vital.

You've seen me grow up and marked all I've done – no day passed by uncounted, slipped by unnoticed. What you think of me matters to me, O God, more than anything else – how much you know about me! (Psalm 139:13-18, WQ, p. 403-404)

For this was shown: that our life is rooted and grounded in love, and that without love we cannot live. . . . For although we poor creatures feel debates and strife within ourselves, yet we are all mercifully enfolded in the gentleness of God – in his kindness, his benignity, his goodwill. (RDL, Chapter 49)

The gift of the Spirit

All over the world and in every Christian community there are people who are talking about receiving the blessing of *the gift of the Holy Spirit*. Protestant, Catholic, Orthodox, some amongst all these followers of Jesus are speaking about this kind of experience. Often they tell of how such a gift was bestowed in a dramatic way. They fell down and/or they began to speak in tongues. Those who, like myself, have not known this experience directly and personally, have almost certainly met those who have. Some speak in extreme language which tends to repel but others display the *fruits of the Spirit* in ways that cannot be ignored. Amongst these fruits are . . .

Awareness. There is a wonderful sense of the reality of Jesus. He is a living person. One to whom they relate in a personal and intimate way.

Sensitivity. They are very sensitive to their own needs and to the needs of others. They have a very real desire to help people with various forms of sickness, drug addiction, alcoholism. They believe that a supernatural power is available to heal and renew and they do see many people helped towards newness of life.

Guidance. They believe that they are guided by God in every detail of their lives. Sometimes what they say about this is almost frightening to many of us. But they do have some remarkable stories to tell.

Talk to people who have been helped by Pentecostal friends and those associated with the charismatic movement. We may not necessarily walk along similar pathways to God but each and every one of us needs to seek and find in our own way *the gift of the Holy Spirit*.

Of course there are dangers, the main one of which is to become totally reliant upon the outward phenomena. To avoid this it is always good to be reminded that the greatest of all the Holy Spirit's gifts is that of love.

> *To each one of us God gives his Spirit in our hearts in one particular way for the good of everybody. . . . But the one same Spirit – God's presence in our hearts – is at work in all these gifts, and God gives them to each of us, one by one, as he thinks best.*
> *(1 Corinthians 12:11, NW, p. 270)*

> *So he says this: Pray inwardly, even though you find no joy in it. For it does good even though you feel nothing, see nothing – yes, even though you think you cannot pray. When you are dry and empty, sick and weak, your prayers please me – though there be little enough to please you. All believing prayer is precious to me.*
> *(RDL, Chapter 41)*

Spirituality and medicine

Where will the next developments in modern medicine be seen? Will it be in the further control and cure of cancer? Many significant developments took place in the last two decades of the twentieth century. There is surely more to come. Will it be in the treatment of Multiple Sclerosis or Motor-Neurone Disease? Many sufferers would be delighted if this were to happen. There are those who are thinking, however, that the next significant development may be in the greater understanding of the relationship between medicine and spirituality.

It has long been acknowledged that there is a direct link between the inner workings of the mind and the strength and vitality of the body. This relates specifically to the ways in which the immune system plays its part in maintaining health and strength. Now, at the highest levels in medical education, it is being recognised that spiritual factors also play an important part. If a person who becomes a patient has inward resources which have provided him or her with a sense of meaning and purpose in life; if they have a sense of being at one with God's plan and supported by God's love, this makes a tremendous difference to the whole person.

A senior Consultant in the NHS who happens also to be a non-stipendary Anglican Priest was asked about the part played by the spiritual in the healing process. He replied: 'I have learnt that when the Spirit of God touches and penetrates the human spirit, there is no limit to the responses the body can make.'

Ian is a retired minister like myself. We were fellow students and friends at college in the late 1940s. A few years ago his kidneys ceased to function and he was placed on dialysis treatment so that the blood could be cleansed from impurities by artificial means. It was an arduous and difficult process involving many hours of care on the part of numerous other people than himself. Then something remarkable happened. His kidneys began to function again and dialysis was no longer necessary. When speaking to his consultant about it, Ian said: 'I believe that what has happened to me is the result of a combination of good medical care and the prayer and spiritual support I have received from so many of my Christian friends.' The good Doctor could only agree.

I don't believe that God has to be persuaded to help his needy ones by a multiplicity of prayers and petitions. I believe that when we pray for ourselves and for others we are seeking to link in with the natural spiritual energies which are an essential part of the make-up of our universe and all who live in it. Relax. Be still. Let go – and let God.

> *If your friendship with me is a real friendship – you in me and I in you – it will bear a great harvest; but there will be no harvest at all if our friendship is broken – you need me.*
> *(John 15:3-5, NW, p. 338)*

> *And notwithstanding that our Lord God dwells in us, and is here with us, and that he beholds us and enfolds us in his tender love and that he is nearer to us than tongue can tell or heart can think . . .*
> *(RDL, Chapter 72)*

Loving my neighbour

My neighbour is any person I know who has some kind of need. It may be that they are lonely, afraid of life, unable to make satisfactory relationships easily. It makes a great difference when I enter their lives and begin to *get the feel* of what is going on inside them. How cheered they are when they realise that someone cares for them and feels for them in their deepest needs.

When I was in my late teens I was trying to discover a pattern for my life and I was anxious to know how to deal with some of the conflicting emotions that kept erupting from within myself. I was fortunate enough to meet a Christian minister at that time who was passing through a difficult period himself. It was wartime and as a convinced pacifist he could not do other than express his convictions. This caused alienation from some members of his congregation. His sharing his anxiety with me enabled me to open up to him. He listened and that in itself was often enough. As I shared with him I felt inward burdens being lifted and new insights seemed just to come. His caring friendship led me in my own search for a vocation – and the psychologists would be sure that his friendship led me into that same Christian ministry. What of it? He was surely God's messenger for me at that time of my life.

However, some of those needy people are extremely hard to like. Also they may cling to us like limpets and make our own lives very difficult. Somehow we have to find a middle way between opting out and not letting one awkward relationship dominate our lives. Of course some difficult 'neighbours' may, by their attitudes, be saying something to us about ourselves. We often react badly with those who are of similar personality traits to ourselves. So difficult relationships, when persevered with in a disciplined way, can contribute towards our own development and growth as persons.

So loving my neighbour can be reasonably easy when my neighbour is someone I get on well with. The demanding truth is, however, that the ones we do not naturally take to may have the deepest needs. Here is a word from Jean Vanier, the founder of L'Arche, a community helping the handicapped and disabled:

> 'To love is not to give of your riches, but to reveal to others their riches, their gifts, their value, and to trust them and their capacity to grow.'

> *But note this; don't let your freedom become an excuse for doing just what you feel like doing. With God's love in your hearts, be ready to do anything – and I mean anything – for one another. For all religion can be put in a single sentence: 'Love the next person as you love yourself.'*
> *(Galatians 5:13-14, NW, p. 266)*

> *. . . it is his will that we should understand that not only does he take care of great and noble things, but also of little and humble things, simple and small – both one and the other. And that is what he means when he says 'all manner of things shall be well'. For he wants us to understand that the smallest thing shall not be forgotten.*
> *(RDL, Chapter 32)*

Worship and worth-ship _____

I was about 28 years old and I was standing on a soap box in the Birmingham Bull Ring sharing, with fellow students, in an open-air meeting largely based on questions and answers. One of the regular questioners challenged me about the purpose of acts of Christian worship. Does your God really require of all his believing subjects that week by week and almost hour by hour people from all over the world tell him what a wonderful God he is?

I ask for your understanding when I admit that whilst I remember the question very well indeed, I cannot remember much about the answer I attempted to give. So let me assume that the same question is being addressed to me now – some forty-nine years later! If Christian worship was simply telling God what a wonderful person he is – full stop – then it is hard to see how its ongoing practice is justified. But there is much more involved. Christian worship is based on the conviction that God, the Creator and Supreme Being, has made himself known to us in Jesus Christ. Worship is our way of responding to this truth and the main purpose of worship is to get to know God better and to seek to ally ourselves with him and his will for our lives, both individually and corporately. The purpose of worship is to be more able to enjoy God and when you do this you have something to thank him for.

But I can almost hear you saying that all this sounds nice but it is far from the reality of our own experience where worship is often dull and so very familiar that we are pleased when each formal act of worship comes to an end.

Here are three suggestions –

Cultivate the habit of not relying on the celebrant or preacher. Take your own real self into each act of worship you attend and look for one simple aspect of understanding or challenge which you did not possess before the service began.

Take one part of your life for which you are grateful and weave that into the pattern of the service.

Years ago I complained to my Franciscan 'father in God' that I was totally bored by the multiplicity of words in the many Psalms which were a staple diet of Franciscan worship. 'Let them just pour over you', was his reply, 'but pick up a word here and a phrase there and hide it in your heart. It will come in useful one day.' I did – and it has!

> *God is good. Men can trust his steadfast love as generation follows generation, for ever!*
> *(Psalm 100:5, WQ, p. 394)*

> *We should pray to our Lord to fear God reverently, and to love him humbly, and to trust him strongly. For the more and stronger we trust, the more we please and honour our Lord we trust in.*
> *(RDL, Chapter 74)*

Stationary pilgrimage

A pilgrim, according to the dictionary, is 'one who is going somewhere in fulfilment of a vow'. This implies movement. If I am a pilgrim I have a destination in mind and I am moving steadily but surely towards that goal.

I have always had to struggle with a racing mind that tends to move quickly from one thing to another. Concentration I have always found difficult especially in prayer. However a watershed experience came to me in middle life for which I shall always be grateful. It was an invitation to attend a meditation group held at a Roman Catholic religious community every Friday evening. It lasted at most three quarters of an hour and consisted of music – a brief introduction – and then silence. The silence was facilitated because each person present was encouraged to have their own sentence which they repeated silently to themselves. This helped to keep the wandering thoughts at bay and encouraged inner stillness. My self-chosen sentence was 'Be still and know that I am God'. The Franciscan Brother Ramon gives some sound advice in his book, *The Heart of Prayer*.[1] 'If there is an invasion of the mind by 101 distracting thoughts, don't fight them, simply return to your sentence prayer. Without strain or fear simply return to your prayer.'

This I have tried to do with varying degrees of success and failure. I used to think it would get easier as one grows older but for me it doesn't, yet I struggle on. After all I am a pilgrim. I am going somewhere. The wisdom of this insight is that in order to facilitate my pilgrimage I must from time to time become stationary. I must 'be still' in order to be able to go on!

1 Published by Marshall Pickering in 1995.

Monica Furlong has written a poem she has entitled 'The Key of the Kingdom'. In it she described a journey that moves inward from the city to the street, to the lane, to the yard, to the house, to the room, to the bed . . . 'And on that bed a basket of sweet flowers'. At the heart of all there is beauty, serenity, peace. But the inward journey must now be taken in reverse, from the bed back to the city. The treasure discovered in 'the basket of sweet flowers' must now be shared with men and women 'in the city'.

This then is the pattern of my 'stationary pilgrimage'. It is an essential part of my journey towards a greater wholeness in Christ.

> *Love is never in a hurry . . . Love holds good –*
> *everywhere, for everybody, for ever.*
> *(1 Corinthians 13:4, 13, NW, p. 272)*

> *At this time he showed how frail we are, and how we*
> *fall; how we are broken and count for nothing . . .*
> *And at the same time he showed his blessed strength,*
> *his blessed wisdom, his blessed love.*
> *(RDL, Chapter 62)*

This is the way I am _____

Have you ever said this to yourself or to someone else: 'Sorry, but this is the way I am . . . I was like this in the beginning . . . am now and ever shall be . . . you must take me or leave me . . . I can't change!'

Surely this is a totally defeatist attitude. Isn't the Christian faith all about change? Isn't that what being *born again* means? Yes, the Christian faith is about change; it is about new life; it is about new understanding. But those changes often come about within the limitations imposed by the experiences which shaped you. So I have made two discoveries which have made a great deal of difference to my life. The first is that I must accept myself as I really am but that this is the gateway to change and the growing ability to adjust positively to what happens to me as my life proceeds. The negative aspects of life can be handled by my facing anxiety or jealousy (yes, it does happen) by my saying to myself: 'Howard, you are at it again.' This in itself is a source of relief.

The second is that as I have gained this insight into my condition I can lay it all out before God during my times of prayer and meditation. I have been aided in this down the years by keeping a diary in which some of the more difficult periods of my life have been spelt out in writing. These can then become the raw material of my deeper understanding of what is happening to me. The end of this process is often thanksgiving.

As I write this piece I recall an incident from yesterday. A man who was left disabled by polio at an early age and needs two sticks to enable him to walk had been at a service I was conducting. I had been preaching about discovering an ongoing spirituality that enables and facilitates our healing and our ability to move on to become more whole as persons. He told me how that at one stage his consultant had called members of the medical team to gather round his bed and he had said to them, 'I want you to look at this man; he is a miracle.' The miracle was not that his patient had been able to get rid of the inheritance left to him by his polio. It lay in the way he had tackled his disability and had lived the fullest of lives within its limitations – and this included an active working life as a farmer.

My biblical passage had been John 5:1-10 – The Vine and the Branches. He, Jesus, is the true vine – as we abide in him so his life flows to us and we can change even within the limitations of our physical, mental and emotional inheritance.

> *In a word, the good news tells us how God puts right what is wrong and how he helps all men everywhere to put wrong things right.*
> *(Romans 1:16-17, NW, p. 252)*

> *And this is how every soul should think inwardly of its lover; that is to say, the love of God makes such a bond between us that, when this is seen truly, no man can separate himself one from another.*
> *(RDL, Chapter 65)*

Reconciliation

Reconciliation is a lovely word. It rolls off the tongue. It is used to describe a new start in interpersonal relations but also a new experience in communal understanding. This always implies an honest attempt to see a divisive issue from the other side.

Years ago I was deeply disappointed by the attitude of the local vicar in whose parish my church was situated. I felt that he regarded me as a lesser human being and certainly not an equal in terms of representing the Church in the civic life of our community. One day he stopped me in the street and enquired why the Bishop of the Diocese had been a visitor to the Methodist Synod which had been held in my Church. 'I'll have you know', he said, 'that your church is in my parish and my permission should have been sought.' I couldn't help myself I'm afraid and replied to him by saying: 'Indeed, well you know, Vicar, John Wesley claimed the world as his parish so that could mean that actually your church is in mine!' He was not amused. I really did try hard to get alongside him and opened up to him regarding my concern about our inability to work together and how it was affecting ecumenical relations. But I was rejected.

Happily I have known other experiences. One man with whom I had sought and found reconciliation felt he had to describe what had happened in a Church meeting: 'Howard invited me into his study and offered me tea and pork pies.' There had also been tears as we each began to appreciate how the other had felt about the breakdown in relationships. Tears can often build bridges when they are genuine and sincere.

What has happened to the whole human race through the death of Jesus on the cross? Potentially there has been opened up the possibility of reconciliation. It all begins by our being friends of Jesus and then seeking friendship of others in his name. This is what then word reconciliation really means – to become a friend.

It was the saint, Catherine of Genoa, who said: 'My me is God nor do I know my selfhood save in him.' This surely is the way forward. As we take the initiative in an act of reconciliation we are getting nearer to becoming our true selves.

> *In Jesus, God is making everybody, everywhere, his friends; and he's not going to list the wrong and unkind things we have done and hold them against us. He wants us to take this message of friendship to others.*
> *(2 Corinthians 5:18-20, NW, p. 268)*

> *. . . we ought to know that the greatest deed has already been done . . . and by thinking this with thankful hearts we ought to pray for the deed that is being done now – and that is that he governs and guides us to worship him in this life and to bring us to his joy. For this reason he has done all the rest.*
> *(RDL, Chapter 41)*

The need to wonder

We who have just moved into a new millennium year have seen many wonders: space travel; moon landings; transplant surgery. Only this morning I have heard of a camera which can be contained within the coating of a pill that can be swallowed and will then transmit pictures of all the organs through which it passes! A godsend for diagnosis of problems in the small bowel was how one commentator described it!! I have completely forgotten where and from whom I heard the following sentence but it is an apt play upon words – 'Our need is not for more wonders but for more wonder.'

Recalling this sentence reminded me of another whose originator I do remember. It was the late Archbishop William Temple who said, 'The world can only be saved by worship.' What an odd claim to make. I can almost hear the politicians and some philosophers pouring scorn upon it. Yet it is worthy of serious thought. We are so used to having all our problems solved. We want instantaneous solutions to the difficulties we are having either with our bodies or with our cars. This is perfectly natural but we must beware of losing the ability to be lost 'in wonder, love and praise'.

I have discovered that the ability to discover inner quietness leads to a sharpening of the ability to appreciate beauty in birds, animals, trees, flowers, but most of all views from heights. Recently we visited a spot we used to know well through living nearby. It was Loweswater in the Lake District. One morning we managed to reach the top of a fell at about 1500 feet. At one time we could climb much higher but not these days. However, we were high enough to see all around us. The Lake, Loweswater village itself; a glimpse of one end of Crummock Water with fells and mountains falling away in the distance. They were majestic moments when we just wanted to stand and stare. Since then those moments of vision have come back to us again and again.

Reflect now on a slightly longer passage from Alan Dale:

Bless God, O my soul! My God how great you are, clothed in splendour and majesty, clothed with light; stretching out the sky like a tent, laying the foundations in the Great Deep; driving the dark storm as your chariot, riding on the clouds as your horses – the winds your heralds, the lightenings your ministers! . . . How many things you have made, O God, made in your wisdom, crowding the earth . . . I will sing to God as long as I live. I will sing his praise all my days! Bless God, O my soul. Praise God!
(From Psalm 104, WQ, pp. 385-7)

Therefore I needs must grant that everything that is done is done well, for it is God that does all. For he is the still point at the centre.
(RDL, Chapter 11)

The valley of tears _____

As a young Minister I soon came face to face with human tragedies: terrible accidents; moral failures; unexpected illness and disease, family breakdowns. I always felt helpless and quite unable to cope. I would just be there and hold on to these shattered people, often just physically embracing them or just holding on to a hand. At that time I thought that as I gained more pastoral experience I would get better at this particular aspect of the job – but I never did. Even today in such situations words and explanations just fail me. When a soul in deep distress cries out 'My God – why?' I still have to say 'I don't know why – but I will stay with you as long as you want me.'

A small family, a man, his wife and 20-year-old daughter were faced with the father and husband's impending death through a terminal illness. The daughter refused to face the reality of what was happening. She would not talk about it and tried to arouse false hopes. The mother was a rather faint-hearted and timorous believer and her circle of churchgoing friends tried to shield her from the real situation with thin spiritual platitudes. Happily – yes that is the word I mean – the husband and father who was dying refused to allow them to deal with what was happening by resorting to trivialities and religious clichés. He insisted that the situation be faced. That plans be made for their lives when he had died. His own beliefs were not strong. He did not know what lay beyond the experience of death except that he felt sure that love would survive in some way or another.

His insistence that reality be faced paid off in that as they nursed him through his final illness they began to realise that they also would die one day but now they had to die to their total dependence upon him; they had to discover resources to cope with the reality of their situation. When he died and they said goodbye they realised that through his insistence on their facing up to the situation they had been saved from being self-centred and totally dependent upon him for all the major decisions of their lives. They passed through 'the valley of tears' but began to experience the promise of Psalm 84 verse 6 that even this dark valley could become 'the place of springs'.

We recently revisited a former church and met an old friend who is now suffering from Alzheimer's disease. It was sad to see him so different to the virile, active man we had known. But we were struck by the way the whole church had responded to the situation. The love and compassion which had been released was another illustration of the 'valley of tears' becoming 'the place of springs'.

I've been in some tight corners – but never cornered; I've lost my way but never my courage; I've been on the run but never left to my fate; I've been knocked down – but never knocked out.
(1 Corinthians 11:24-29, NW, p. 190)

The trouble is this – that the range of our thinking is now so blinkered, little and small, that we cannot see the high and wonderful wisdom and power and goodness of the blessed Trinity. And this is what he means when he says 'You shall see for yourself that all manner of things will be well.' It is as if he said: 'Have faith and have trust, and, at the last day you shall see it all transformed into great joy.'
(RDL, Chapter 32)

Come alive

On a memorable occasion I shared in a meeting with the late Archbishop Michael Ramsey. He had come to answer students' questions at a regional College of Technology where I was one of the chaplains. I was afraid that this scholarly academic might not go down well with the aggressive students I knew many of them to be. I need not have worried. He won their respect and indeed their admiration first by the way he showed his respect for them and then by his total honesty. He did not claim to have all the answers and he shared his real self with them. He came across as a living human being who was in love with life and in love with God. I learnt that day . . .

1. People who are truly alive know and experience conflict.
Discerning conflict is a direct sign that we are alive. Conflict is about internal debate. It is about promoting and encouraging challenges from within oneself. They can be of many kinds. It is encouraging to know that Jesus himself experienced inner conflict especially in the Garden of Gethsemane . . . 'Father, if it be possible, let this cup pass from me, nevertheless thy will, not mine be done.' Paul experienced conflict: 'The good that I would do, I do not; but the evil which I would not that I do.' Living within the Jesus orbit will reveal the shadows within. Such experiences are life giving; they make for growth and development.

2. People who are truly alive will sometimes feel lost.
I have often been wholly dependent upon human support. My spiritual stock has been low, indeed, I have felt empty. Human friendship has seen me through but almost inevitably after a dry season God has sent someone or some book – or even a sermon (sometimes my own) – and I have been found again. I am back.

3. People who are truly alive share their 'aliveness' quite naturally.
She presided over a healing service in her elongated wheelchair. She was paralysed. Her hair fell in long tresses by her side. She had begun this service years ago and now every month a hundred or so people came to this remote Cornish village church. She was truly alive. She sparkled. She was radiant. I had to go to her and ask that she lay her hands upon me. She did and she shared her life with me. Her Christ life. It was a truly living experience.

> *. . . when the time was ripe, God sent his Son to live among us as one of us to help us to live as his sons and daughters, grown up members of his family. Because this is what we now are, he has given us the spirit of his Son in our hearts.*
> *(Galatians 4:4-7, NW, p. 268)*

> *He wills that we trust him, and understand him, and know that he is Life. And he wills that our understanding is rooted in this with all our strength, and will, and reason, so that this ground becomes our home and dwelling place.*
> *(RDL, Chapter 42)*

Water

My car is in dock. Whilst waiting for the repair to be completed I am given a glass of cool, sparkling water. I begin to think about water in relation to my car. First of all it cools. It has to be mixed with anti-freeze but it circulates around the engine helping to keep the processes cool and so functional. Only once have I had a radiator leak. Then, devoid of water, my car overheated and stopped.

I need to be cooled. I overheat and hinder my proper functioning as a person. My nerves jangle. My head aches. I cannot think properly because my mind is racing from one subject to another. I stop and listen and a voice out of the Bible says to me: 'Whoever believes in me, streams of living water will pour out from his heart.' I use my own internal disciplinary powers to visualise that happening to me – now.

> Breathe through the heat of *my* desire,
> thy coolness and thy balm.
>
> *John Greenleaf Whittier*

Then there is a large tank of water that is for cleaning purposes. At a touch of the appropriate button water is sprayed on the windscreen and the wipers function and clear my vision. On dirty, rainy nights or when spray is being thrown up on to my windscreen by lorries, the cleansing water is vital for my safety.

I need to be cleansed. I get soiled. Other people's dirt rubs off on me. I fail to respond to a challenge to be more compassionate; to be more loving. I am selfish and find myself putting more emphasis on material things than I know is good for me.

> Drop thy still dews of quietness,
> till all *my* strivings cease.
>
> *John Greenleaf Whittier*

The battery is special. A particular kind of water is needed for the occasional top-up. This is *distilled* water from which the impurities have been extracted by the boiling process and a more pure water results. This is now suitable for the operating of the battery which then provides power to starter motor, lights, wipers and a number of other functioning parts.

I need power. Power to live. Water provides power. Steam engines now are few and far between but for generations of men and women they were a major means of transport. All over the world water power is harnessed to provide electricity. But I need inward power to give me motivation, drive and purpose.

> O come and dwell in me,
> Spirit of power within . . .
> *Charles Wesley*

Hi! You who are thirsty come and drink. . . . You don't need money – everything is free.
(Isaiah 55:1, WQ, p. 295)

And he should carry on his work . . . and make sweet streams flow, and noble and plentiful fruit to spring forth.
(RDL, Chapter 51)

Merton

In a previous piece I have already referred to Thomas Merton. He was a spiritual giant. The story of his life and his growth and development as a humane, human being was told by him in his autobiography *The Seven Story Mountain*. But that was not the only telling of his story. Another account was given by the British writer, broadcaster and journalist, Monica Furlong. I have just been rereading her book entitled simply *Merton – a biography*.[1] To read about the inner trials and torments through which he passed in the course of his own personal psychological development including his struggle with neurotic symptoms, was music in my ears. I felt at home.

I was particularly drawn to Monica Furlong's description of the real Merton . . . 'He began to see that the highest spiritual development was to be *ordinary*, to be fully a man, in the way few human beings succeed in becoming so simply and nat-urally themselves. He began to see the monk not, as he had believed in his youth, as someone special, undertaking feats of incredible ascetic heroism for the love of God, but as one who was not afraid to be simply *man*.' Merton lived with a deep awareness of his natural appetites which he saw as contribut-ing to his manhood. He did not attempt to repress or deny his basic human needs; to acknowledge them openly was the first step towards dealing with them constructively.

I warmed to this. To be a Christian means different things to different people. For some it just means being born in a nominally Christian country. For others it means to have been baptised into the Christian Faith. Then there are those who have discovered what they believe to be *real Christianity*. They have been *born again*. I do not denigrate such revolutionary

1 Published by Collins in 1980.

experiences. I have known personally many individuals who have come alive in this way. Sadly, however, there are those for whom religion takes over. They become obsessed by its terminology; its own kind of spiritual language. They need constant shots in the arm of religious enthusiasm. They deny and repress real aspects of their own personhood.

Michael Ramsey comes back into my mind. He once wrote, 'Nature will not be discarded, in order that men's souls alone may be salvaged and saved . . . rather all that God has made will have its place and its counterpart in the new heaven and the new earth.' (Quote discovered in my commonplace book.)

As I recall all that I have written above I feel my heart to be *strangely warmed*.

> *Come here to me all you who are tired with hard work. I will put new life into you. I will give you a hand and show you how to live. I'll go your pace and see you through – and I'll give you the secret of a quiet mind.*
> *(Matthew 11:28-30, NW, p. 85)*

> *Our work of prayer and our work of living well – which we do by his grace – both please him. We must direct our strength through him until the time when we have what we seek – that is Jesus in fullness of joy. (RDL, Chapter 41)*

A therapeutic community

I was sharing in a meeting being addressed by the Medical Superintendent of a large hospital for mental and nervous illness. He was describing to us how he was trying to create a different kind of atmosphere in that hospital. He described his aim as being to create a 'therapeutic community'. This would seek to unlock the healing potential each one of us possesses in relation to each other. In a hospital there are many professionals each with their own particular expertise; there are also porters, cleaners, domestic staff, clerical staff and administrators. Finally there are the patients. His case was that the one common factor was the humanity shared by all and the fact that all had needs – including himself – the senior professional among them. He wanted artificial barriers to be broken down – uniform being the prime example. He wanted a greater openness between all the members of that community. No one should hide behind their rank or professional qualifications. Everyone should be available.

Another doctor, this time a cancer specialist, was trying to achieve something similar and held regular meetings between patients, staff at all levels – and patients' relatives. He described it in an article in the *Observer* as seeking to create a 'bucket of love' into which all may contribute and from which all may draw.

My immediate reaction was that this is exactly what the local church should ideally be – a therapeutic community which is 'a bucket of love'. I then began to think about the different communities I have belonged to both inside and outside the Church. Which were the ones which had helped me most? This was not a difficult question to answer. They were those which had given me love and acceptance and created an atmosphere where I did not have to wear a mask but could really be myself.

I was helping with a church weekend at a delightful conference centre on the south coast. The young minister told me that he was planning a 'late-night extra'. About half those present came. He had put a small low table in the centre of a circle of easy chairs. On the table was one lighted candle. The lights were switched off and he invited anyone to say anything that was on their hearts or to offer a short prayer – or just to be quiet. There was a long healing silence then one lady told of how she had come to that church years ago when she had been deserted by her husband. She wanted to thank them for their love and friendship. This released something in our midst and several others spoke openly about personal matters of concern; others offered short prayers. It was a meaningful experience and I remember saying to some of them afterwards: 'Isn't this what the Church should always be – a truly therapeutic community – a bucket of love?'

> *They were one in heart and mind, and none of them thought that his own things were just for his own use. So the friends of Jesus, like Peter, made it really clear what 'Jesus being alive again' really meant.*
> *(Acts 2:44-47, NW, p. 142)*

> *And then I saw that every feeling of kinship and compassion that a man feels, in love, for his fellow Christians, it is Christ within him.*
> *(RDL, Chapter 28)*

Creative disappointment

I first began to write articles for publication when I was in my early thirties. Let me be honest about my motivation. We had two children and stipends were proportionately lower than they are today. We were very poor and I needed a little more cash. Writing seemed one option. What an uphill struggle it was. The brown SAEs came tumbling through the letterbox with annoying regularity. I was on the point of giving up when a more accomplished writer to whom I had gone for advice said to me, 'When you get an article back, don't bin it right away. Go through it line by line and imagine that you are the editor of the paper or magazine who has returned it. Ask yourself if it fits in with the ethos of that particular journal. Then revise it and send it back with an explanatory letter.' I did and soon a little success began to come my way.

Since then I have discovered that often, within disappointments there is valuable experience to be gained. I spoke on the telephone to a lady who was faced with a situation involving other people than herself. She desperately wanted to act as mediator and reconciler and had tried hard but she had been rejected by all concerned. I felt led to suggest to her that perhaps she wasn't the right person to act as mediator. Perhaps she should consider withdrawing from the scene; hand it over prayerfully to God and pray that others might come forward. It was hard for her to do – but in the end she accepted my advice.

There have been times when I have been disappointed. Jobs I would have liked did not come my way. Gifts I honestly believed were mine were not being used to the full. From time to time I wanted desperately to be delivered from the routine chores of the job I was doing at that time. God's remedy, which became mine, was to turn to those tasks I found most difficult of all – and get on with them. I can honestly say now that I have discovered more about myself and more about God from failure than from success.

Yes, and I am in good company. Thomas was disappointed because he had not been there when others had 'seen the Lord'. Peter let Jesus down because things were not going as he wanted. One of Paul's friends, Demas, let him down as Paul declares, 'Demas hath forsaken me, having loved this present world.' Thomas and Peter worked through their disappointments. As far as I know Demas did not! How about you?

> *I've tried to live as Jesus lived. He was sincere in all he did; he knew what he stood for; he could put up with anything; he didn't just talk about loving people – he actually succeeded in loving them; he always told people the plain truth, for he knew that God was with him and trusted in God's power. I've tried to live like that.*
> *(Colossians 1:28-29, NW, p. 195)*

> *For we are his heavenly treasure and he looks on us with so much love while we are here on earth that he wants to give us more light and comfort in heavenly joy by drawing our hearts to him from our sorrow and darkness.*
> *(RDL, Chapter 86)*

Possessions

We all have them. Some have more than others but we all possess some 'things' which are of value. Also there are people who matter a great deal to us. If we lost them either through death or in some other way, we should feel utterly bereft.

Possessions, whether things or people, have to be carefully possessed. We are 'stewards' and this implies wise and careful management. I think I know what John Wesley meant when he said, 'Earn all you can – save all you can – give all you can', although sometimes 'saving' can become an obsession – especially when you are growing older and you wonder how you are going to manage if and when you cannot care adequately for yourself. Being in the later stages of life myself I want to try to achieve a proper kind of balance which takes seriously our Lord's command to 'love my neighbour as myself.'

Here is a verse written by Father William Hewitt. It is part of a song:

> Know in your life what last and grows,
> choose the better way he shows.
> Don't grab everything, whoever can?
> Discern what will last – and choose God's love in man.

I can recall an occasion when a certain family in one of my churches tried to possess me. They have long since gone or I would not tell the story. It began almost immediately on arrival by their saying to my wife and I: 'We have always been the minister's best friends.' Then came invitations and gifts and suggestions about what should and should not happen in our church. Suddenly I realised that I was being 'bought'. The couple in question were trying to possess me. I had to make it clear in the nicest of ways that I was everybody's friend. Some parents try to possess their children beyond the days of their proper independence. Some even try to live their lives through their children. It never works and often produces the opposite effect to what is desired – relationships break down. It is always good to remember the words of the Psalmist: 'To God belongs the earth and all it holds, the world and all who live in it' (Psalm 24:1).

Do not store up for yourselves treasure on earth, where moth and worm eat things up, where thieves break through and steal. Store up for yourselves treasure in heaven, where no moth or worm eats things up, where no thieves break into houses and steal. For heart and treasure go together.
(Matthew 6:19-21, NW, p. 87)

A cheerful giver does not count the cost of what he gives. His heart is set on pleasing him to whom the gift is given. And if he who receives it takes the gift with joyful thanks, then the courteous giver thinks it has cost him nothing compared with the joy and happiness he has had in pleasing and delighting the one he loves.
(RDL, Chapter 23)

On being unique

Those who regularly commit crimes know that fingerprint evidence has often been the means of prosecution and conviction. So they wear gloves and do their best to clean up any kind of trace of their presence at the scene of a crime. Now they have another hazard to contend with – especially when physical contact has been made with another person as in cases of assault. Now the smallest molecule from their living person can provide DNA evidence. If this can be matched with samples taken from themselves a prosecution can be brought which it is difficult to defend.

These are but two indications of the total uniqueness of each human being. Now take this a stage further. There are some contributions to the common life of the community, and to the lives of certain individuals, that only we can make. If we opt out; if we turn the challenge aside, the life of our community and the lives of some individuals will be all the poorer.

The responsibility is frightening but there is no need to shrink from the various tasks because of their magnitude. All that we do in the name of Jesus he *accomplishes through us*. We are the channels. The work is his – but he does require our active co-operation.

Remember St Teresa's oft-quoted words: 'Christ has no body now on earth but yours, no hands but yours, no feet but yours. Yours are the eyes through which Christ's compassion looks out to the world. Yours are the feet through which he is to go about doing good. Yours are the hands through which he is to bless men now.'

You can buy sparrows five a penny; yet God keeps his eye on every sparrow. He counts every hair of your head. There's nothing to fear: you mean more to him than a flock of sparrows.
(Luke 12:6, NW, p. 83)

And this is the joy of Christ's works, and this is what he means when he says that we are his joy, we are his reward, we are his glory, we are his crown.
(RDL, Chapter 31)

Taizé and Iona

These two places have had an influence on my life. I have never been to Taizé but I have been to Iona just once. As long ago as 1974 I was captured by the message sent by 40,000 young people gathered at Taizé to the whole Church of Christ. It became part of my vision of what I dearly longed for the Church to be. This was the heart of that message: 'Are you at last going to become a universal community of sharing . . . a place of community and friendship for the whole of humanity? Are you going to become the people of the beatitudes, having no security other than Christ, a people poor, contemplative, creating peace, bearing joy and a liberating festival for mankind?' This message was encapsulated in their music. Somehow it was different. I recall the first time I heard 'Jesus remember me when I come into your Kingdom'. It was played and sung by some students in between intercessory prayers at a major conference. Since then I have used many different Taizé choruses and chants, from the Gloria to the Nunc Dimittis, especially as part of Quiet Days and Retreats. Through Taizé songs I have been brought nearer to God.

And what of Iona? Music again comes to mind. Sunday morning worship in the abbey church. Praise that rose spontaneously from hundreds of voices. Plain exposition of the word of God applied directly to the lives we live and the world we live in. This to me is the significance of Iona, the direct relevance of the message lived out in community and applied to every aspect of life. I recall the illustration used by the founder, Dr George McLeod, of the stained glass window bearing the message, *Glory to God in the Highest*. One letter had disappeared, broken and scattered by a stone. Now the message read, *Glory to God in the High st*. This was where the vitality of the gospel was to be tested. Where men and woman meet together for the ordinary business of living, personal Christian experience and the struggle for social justice must always go hand in hand. Iona, in my judgement, has got the balance right. I use their songs, their poems, their dramatic excerpts, etc., constantly as I lead worship in different churches and they are always appreciated.

From time to time I have to ask myself a serious question – does my acceptance of the message of Jesus and my consequent involvement with the Christian Church protect me from real life or expose me to it? I mean this with all seriousness. Church life can become a kind of cocoon; a protective shield; it can almost be like membership of a very respectable club. It is good to be reminded that we follow a Lord who died on a cross with a thief on either side. You cannot get more down to earth than that.

'The man who loves me', said Jesus, 'will take what I say seriously. My Father will love him, and we will come to him and make our home in his heart.'
(John 14:21, NW, p. 337)

Love was his meaning. Who showed it to you? Love. What did he show you? Love. Why did he show you? For love. Hold fast to this and you shall learn and know more about love.
(RDL, Chapter 86)

Life beyond death

In a truly remarkable way Jesus found fulfilment through his death and resurrection. Deep within each one of us is the desire to be fulfilled. This is good. It provides the motivation to keep on searching for truth and enlightenment.

In our dying there is fulfilment. What we do not know is the nature of that fulfilment. In *Silas Marner*, Silas is only concerned about his gold. This is his satisfaction. In getting more he believes that he is fulfilled. Then it is stolen and his only concern is to find the robber and get it back. But instead a golden haired girl comes into his home and he grows to love her and eventually adopt her. This proves to be the source of a more real and lasting fulfilment but one which was totally unexpected.

In our dying there is completion. God's loving purpose for us will be accomplished. This is sometimes hard to recognise when a much loved person suffers, deteriorates and dies before our very eyes. Yet I have seen resurrection begin in such people before they pass over. I have seen the strength and insight given to match the hour of need.

Whilst I was a student in the late forties I benefited greatly from the ministry of a man named Leslie Tizard. He was the minister of the then Carrs Lane Congregational Church in Birmingham. He died from cancer in his late fifties and had the courage to write a book during his last illness which he entitled *Facing Life and Death*. It was a moving book in which you saw a man struggle and strive and then accept the inevitable. I paraphrase something he wrote towards the end: 'I decided to give my life to God rather than that he should take it from me. In the moment of giving I knew peace.'

Resurrection and death are part of the same experience. There can be no resurrection without death neither in our continuing lives nor in our final exit. We see 'through a glass darkly' but in some indefinable way there is given to us the intuition that in death there is life – resurrection life – Christ's life!

> 'Stop worrying,' said Jesus, 'keep trusting God and keep trusting me. There are many different places in my Father's home for people to live. I would have told you long ago if this was not true. I am going away now to make sure that there is a place for you.'
> (John 14:1-3, NW, p. 336)

> So was I taught that love was our Lord's meaning. And I saw full surely that before ever God made us, he loved us. And this love was never quenched, nor ever shall be. ... And in this love our life is everlasting. In our making we had a beginning but the love in which he made us was without beginning. In which love we have our beginning. And all this we shall see in God without end – which Jesus grant us. Amen.
> (RDL, Chapter 86)